May 12, 1992

Dearest Terry —

I "forgive" you for being a Trojan! Thanks so much for the opportunity to learn so much — and to have such a wonderful "holiday"! I owe you!

Love,
Valerie Wohlquist
"Producer AACC 1992"

College Football's Great Dynasties
USC

College Football's Great Dynasties

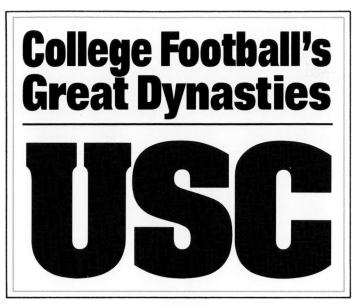

USC

Jack Clary

SMITHMARK

Published by Smithmark Publishers
112 Madison Avenue
New York, New York 10016

Produced by
Brompton Books Corp.
15 Sherwood Place
Greenwich, CT 06830

ISBN 0-8317-3478-7

Printed in Hong Kong

10 9 8 7 6 5 4 3 2 1

PICTURE CREDITS

Chance Brockway: 2, 3, 34, 35(bottom), 37(top),
   38(bottom), 39, 40, 42, 43(bottom), 44, 46,
   47(right), 56, 60-61, 62, 69, 76.
Malcolm Emmons: 6, 7, 45(top), 63.
Bill Mesler Collection: 37(bottom).
Bruce Schwartzman: 54(top).
UPI/Bettmann Archives: 1, 4, 8(both), 9, 11(bottom),
   12(right), 12(left), 13, 15(both), 16, 17(both),
   18(both), 19(both), 20, 21, 22(both), 23, 24, 25(both),
   26, 27, 28, 29(both), 30, 31, 32, 33(both), 35(top),
   36(both), 41(both), 48, 49, 54(bottom), 58, 59(bot-
   tom), 64, 65, 66, 67, 68, 70, 71, 72, 73, 74.
USC: 10, 11(top), 12(left), 13(right), 38(top), 43(top),
   45(bottom), 51(top right & bottom), 59(top), 75, 77.
USC/Greg Cara: 51(top left).
USC/Robert Hagedohm: 52-53.
USC/Jim Lanahan: 50.
USC/Merv Lew: 47(left).
USC/Peter Read Miller: 57.
USC/John Soohoo: 55.

ACKNOWLEDGMENTS

The author had some fine support from Pat Harmon,
librarian and curator at the College Football Hall of
Fame in Kings Island, Ohio, and Joe Horrigan, his
counterpart at Pro Football's Hall of Fame in Canton,
Ohio. Both were most generous in opening their files
and supplying background material for this book.
Two valuable sources were *The Trojans*, by Ken Rap-
paport, and *The Best Little Rivalry in Town* by Jody
Brown. The author also wishes to thank Barbara
Hayes for her work in compiling additional research
material at the University of Southern California,
and to that school's sports information office for its
cooperation. Of course, no author is secure without
the advice and skill of an editor, in this case Jean
Martin of the Bison Group, as well as the talents of
those who helped to put this book together: Sara
Antonecchia, the picture researcher; Don Longa-
bucco, the designer; and Elizabeth A. McCarthy, the
indexer.

Page 1: *Coach John Robinson and tailback Charles White lead the celebration after the Trojans defeated the UCLA Bruins 49-14 to clinch a berth in the 1980 Rose Bowl. White ran for four touchdowns and gained 194 yards for USC.*

Page 2: *Coach Larry Smith prepares his team for the 1989 Ohio State game.*

Page 3: *USC's card section spells out victory in maroon and gold at the 1973 Rose Bowl.*

These pages: *Backfield in motion: (left to right) Homer Griffith, Rod Cameron, Gar Matthews, Bill Howard, and Irving "Cotton" Warburton led the Trojans to a third straight national championship in 1933.*

Contents

Preface

Talk about University of Southern California football and many pleasant and familiar images come to mind: great football stars such as Ernie Pinckert, Cotton Warburton, Jim Sears, Frank Gifford, Jon Arnett, Mike Garrett, Anthony Davis, Ricky Bell, Charles White, Marcus Allen, and of course, The Juice – O.J. Simpson, perhaps the most famous of them all; "student body right and student body left," the famous end sweeps by John McKay's great backs, with a bevy of maroon-clad blockers leading the way and burying any opponents in their path; New Year's Day and the Rose Bowl, including the 1939 game in which Doyle Nave threw a last-minute pass to Al

Right: *Hailed by some as the greatest running back of all time, 1968 Heisman Trophy winner O. J. Simpson helped define Coach John McKay's explosive "student body right and left" offense.*

Opposite: *Two other great USC running backs who made it big in the pros were Heisman Trophy winners Marcus Allen (33) and Charles White (12).*

Above: *Howard Jones provides a bit of hands-on training at practice before his first season as Trojan head coach in 1925. He led USC to 11 victories in 13 games that year, the most wins in a season by any USC team to that time.*

Right: *USC revellers carry off the Victory Bell after defeating UCLA 14-12 in 1952. Both teams were unbeaten going into the game, and, as so often has been the case through the years, the game decided who would go to the Rose Bowl.*

Left: *QB Pete Beathard scrambles for a short gain against Wisconsin at the 1963 Rose Bowl. The top-ranked Trojans pulled off an exciting 42-37 win over the No. 2-ranked Badgers.*

Krueger to beat unbeaten and unscored-upon Duke; great coaches such as Elmer "Gloomy Gus" Henderson, Howard Jones, Jeff Cravath, John McKay, John Robinson, and now Larry Smith, walking the sidelines and directing his players as a conductor would lead his musicians; and, more often than not, total effort rewarded by great success.

Other images also epitomize Southern California football: the Coliseum itself, with its red track, green playing field and multi-colored seats filled with people clad in a rich array of tropical pastels; the familiar steps at the open end of the arena, where ageless columns surround the Olympic flame that has twice been lighted in this century; sun-splashed Saturday afternoons which are so typical of late fall in Southern California and which, thanks to television, stand in sharp contrast to playing conditions in other, frost-encrusted sections of the country; the Hollywood stars sprinkled throughout the tens of thousands of fans who jam the Coliseum each week; the prototypical blonde cheerleaders with their California tans, gorgeous smiles, and enough bounce to revitalize even the most energy-deficient couch potato; the hundreds of musicians dressed as Trojan warriors, looking as if they are right out of central casting; and the inspirational Traveler, the beautiful white horse mascot with a regal Trojan astride.

And, of course, there are the rivalries which reach up and down the Pacific Coast, and even into the Midwest, against Notre Dame. Every year, Southern Cal engages in a battle for bragging rights with its neighbor from Westwood, UCLA, and pursues its unique South versus North encounters against the University of California at Berkeley and Stanford University, both of which have seniority in the game, but not always parity on the field. The rivalry with Notre Dame was born of Knute Rockne who, as his final deed, thrust his team into every section of the United States, and it has always remained special in the minds and hearts of both schools. Some of Southern Cal's greatest victories – and bitterest defeats – have come on fall afternoons in South Bend, Indiana, or at the Coliseum.

All of these things are as much about Southern California football as the long runs and passes, crunching tackles and blocks, and the victories which have accumulated by the hundreds. Indeed, football at USC is as much perception as reality, which befits something that happens almost within shouting distance of the nation's movie-making industry where illusion is the key, and its acceptance is the objective.

There is something special about this atmosphere, something that seems to go against the very nature of football itself which was born amidst falling autumn leaves, cheeks made rosy from crisp air, and often, toes made numb by snow and freezing temperatures. Instead, Southern California plays its football in idyllic conditions, and has always added enough splash and dash to make it distinctive, and reflective of this different section of the country, where life's pace is unique.

But with all of these elements serving as a backdrop tapestry, one thing is unmistakable – Southern California football has always represented the best the college sport has to offer.

1. The Building of Troy Begins

Below: *USC's first football team in 1888: Sitting (from left), Harry Lillie, end; E. E. Reed, center; C. C. Carpenter, end; Frank Davis, tackle; Arthur Carroll, back; Frank Lapham, tackle. Standing: John Norton, guard; Harvey Bailey, back; Will C. Whitcomb, back; J. Edward Young, guard; Frank Suffell, assistant coach; E. E. Hall, back.*

In 1888, Los Angeles was still a bucolic paradise of lush valleys and modest population, a city beginning to emerge. Tucked neatly against the Pacific Ocean and protected by the San Gabriel Mountains from eastern invaders bringing trendy pastimes, Los Angeles had barely been touched by the newfangled form of entertainment called organized sports. A few travelers who had seen thousands jammed into playing fields of the East to watch young men pursue new games called baseball and football had filtered through those natural barriers and spun some wondrous tales of new ways to spend an off-day or flex some youthful muscles. But the idea of pursuing these activities on any such scale in the sleepy Los Angeles of the 1880s seemed very remote indeed.

In 1888, the University of Southern California was just eight years old, with a tiny population that wouldn't even fill some of the school's auditoriums today. There was no Memorial Coliseum; no Tommy Trojan; no tanned, blonde cheerleaders or brightly clad and helmeted band; and no UCLA to kick around; for, as hard as it may seem to believe in this day and age, there was no football as yet at USC.

But the young men of that time were restless and had already begun competition in baseball and track with St. Vincent's College (later Loyola) and Occidental. Finally, in 1888, the "Methodists" as they were nicknamed in those days found some 18 young men, mostly sophomores, who wanted to play football on an organized basis. Those pioneers included John Nor-

SOUTHERN CALIFORNIA VARSITY 1897

Left: Coach Lew Freeman (third from left, standing) led the 1897 "Methodists," as USC was then known, to a 5-1 record. The team included USC's first black player, Robert Jones (left, standing).

Below: Coach Dean Cromwell won 26 games in two stints (1909-10 and 1916-18). During his second tenure, USC became a contender for the first time. Yet, he still is better known for his half-century as track and field coach.

ton, Harvey Bailey, Will Whitcomb, Ed Young, Frank Suffell (assistant coach), Elmer Hall, Harry Lillie, Edgar Reed, C.C. Carpenter, F.E. Davis, Arthur Carroll, Frank Lapham, Tommy Robinson, T.N. Carver and three others whose names have been lost to posterity.

The team colors were purple and gold, but the players had no uniforms as their counterparts had in the East and Midwest. They played in what they chose to wear and against whoever would play them, because there were no organized intercollegiate teams in southern California.

On November 14, 1888, some 19 years after Princeton visited Rutgers to start this great fall tradition, this intrepid group of collegians convinced a group of youths that formed the Alliance Athletic Club in downtown Los Angeles to play a game, and came away with a 16-0 victory in what has always been regarded officially as the school's first game. The second game occurred on January 19, 1889 against the same group and again USC won, 4-0.

No records exist of who scored or how they did it in either game, but the results were official and the seeds of football as a sport at the University had been planted. The sport's development would not be rapid (sometimes there was a drought such as occurred nearly a quarter century later in 1911-13 when the school abandoned intercollegiate football in favor of rugby) because there was little intercollegiate competition in southern California, and the

teams in the northern part of the state, such as those at the University of California at Berkeley and at Stanford, were already well-established and preferred competition elsewhere.

But the same energetic students who had convinced Alliance to play them also spent much of their vacation time that summer working out a match with their counterparts at Loyola that was played just before Thanksgiving. Paul Arnold, formerly a professor at the University, and T.N. Carver, the team's fullback, worked out a series of plays that were so well-rehearsed that Loyola was an easy 40-0 victim. A short time later, Pasadena College challenged Southern Cal, and although their team, comprised mainly of students who had been exposed to the game at eastern colleges, tried to re-create the famed Flying Wedge made popular at Yale, it wasn't even a pale imitation and USC emerged with a 26-0 victory to end its second season.

Harvey Holmes became the school's first salaried coach in 1904, and he produced 19 victories in his four seasons, expanding the schedule to include the team's first venture northward where it lost to Stanford, 16-0, in 1905, the first year in which the school played a 10-game schedule. Until 1915, with home games played at old Bovard Field, the collegiate opposition consisted mainly of Whittier, Occidental, Loyola, Pasadena, Cal Tech, and Pomona, plus an array of high school, service, and athletic club teams.

The team attracted as a two-term coach

Above: *Coach Elmer (Gloomy Gus) Henderson's teams played wide-open, exciting football, and won 45 games in six seasons (1919-24). Henderson also brought USC to its first post-season games, winning the 1923 Rose Bowl over Penn State.*

Above: *A tranquil campus setting at USC during the 1920s, favored for years by Hollywood to portray "typical" American colleges.*

Dean Cromwell, whose greatest legacy to American sports lay in the years ahead when he became the nation's foremost track and field coach. Cromwell was 10-1-3 in 1909-10, and in a second stint from 1916-18, he was 11-5-5. As he proved during his long and distinguished career as a track coach, Cromwell was special. His players said he instilled in them a feeling that they could not be defeated, and that was one of the keys in an upset, scoreless tie against California in 1917.

More than anything, though, Cromwell started USC's football program on an upward spiral. Many believe that he is the catalyst for all of the glory that would become the school's legacy, because by the time he returned as head coach in 1916, football had become a passion on the West Coast and he raised the school's level of competition and excellence to meet that emotional groundswell.

A year before, under coach Ralph Glaze, USC reached out for the first time to embrace strong intercollegiate competition, scheduling games against St. Mary's, Oregon, Utah, and two against Cal-Berkeley. They split with Cal, beat St. Mary's, and lost to Oregon and Utah, but at last the school had shown a willingness to play teams from other parts of the West. It still maintained a rivalry with Occidental, California, and Pomona, but in the next few years Arizona, Oregon State, Stanford, and Nevada were also added.

Cromwell upgraded the sport in other areas when he returned for his second stint in 1916. He established a training table,

oversaw the revitalization of old Bovard Field, and honed the skills of his players as no other USC coach had to that time. His finest player during that time was Frank Mallette, dubbed "The Rabbit" because of his great open field running abilities.

With the program then solidly established, Cromwell turned the coaching reins over to Elmer Henderson, and the first great era of Southern Cal football began from 1919 through 1924, when his teams posted a 45-7 record and won their first Rose Bowl game, 14-3 against Penn State on January 1, 1923. Details of that game are covered in Chapter 8.

Henderson came from Oberlin, Ohio and had played at Oberlin College before carving out a glittering high school coaching record at Broadway High School in Los Angeles. After Navy service during World War I, he was lured to USC when Harry Grayson, a sports writer for the old *Los Angeles Express* and later the nationally renowned sports editor of *Newspaper Enterprises Association*, and *Times* sports editor Mark Kelly, campaigned vigorously to bring a big-time football program to Los Angeles. To do otherwise, they claimed, would blight the community's standing. Grayson made his pitch for Henderson, and the University agreed.

Henderson was aptly nicknamed "Gloomy Gus" because publicly he never professed optimism of any sort. It was a trait that he allegedly inherited from his old trainer at Oberlin ("You boys sure is goin' to get slaughtered because you don't know nothin' about football," was the usual refrain before every Oberlin game). Though Henderson adopted it, he nonetheless was revered by his players who overlooked his gloom-and-doom traits and were positive in everything they did. He was renowned for his fair dealings and his ability to inspire his players through his personal relationships.

As a tactician, Henderson was a man ahead of his time on the West Coast because, despite his Gloomy Gus monicker, he was an imaginative, innovative coach who used a wide open style of play that sent runners and footballs flying in every direction. He used the running game to set up a well-conceived passing game in an era when the pass was not much of a weapon. He carried his great recruiting skills into the Los Angeles area and always attracted talented players who exhibited the flair that his football style required.

Henderson had been a high school coach in Washington State where football was played at a higher level than in southern California, and he brought a fine array of talent with him to USC, enabling the Trojans to win four of five games in 1919, including victories over Stanford and Utah. The first glimpse of financial success also began to peek through as the team sold 850 season tickets, and some 9000 persons turned out for the California game, a tough 14-13 loss for the Trojans who nonetheless proved, with players such as linemen Eddie Simpson, Swede Evans, captain John Fox and Jimmy Smith, plus halfback Charley Dean and fullback Johnny Leadingham, that they could play with the best teams in the West. That team even was considered

for the Rose Bowl berth that eventually went to Oregon.

A year later, in 1920, USC had what can be clearly labeled its first "perfect" season by winning all six games, including a mighty 21-0 victory over the Ducks team that had defeated Harvard in the Rose Bowl, and a third straight victory over Stanford. Things were even better in 1921 when USC won 10 of 11 games (two were against Navy teams representing the battleships *USS Arizona* and *USS New York*, plus two games against a team from the Navy's submarine base at Long Beach). The big game that year saw some 26,000 fans cram California Field in Berkeley, with scalpers getting as much as $15 per ticket. But the Bears were a far superior team with more depth, and romped to a 38-7 victory that helped win them a place in the Rose Bowl. But USC had come far enough to be welcomed into the Pacific Coast Conference, a mark that its football program was truly competitive.

The lessons of 1921 were well-learned because in 1922, Henderson's team won all but its game against California and received its first Rose Bowl invitation. Cal and USC played each other as the inaugural game in the present Rose Bowl stadium and the Golden Bears won 12-0. A crowd of 15,000 turned out for that game; but when USC had defeated Arizona at Bovard Field, the place nearly burst with 12,000 fans, almost double its capacity.

That was a signal that the Trojans needed a more spacious site and the following year, in 1923, they moved to the Los Angeles Coliseum, built on the edge of the

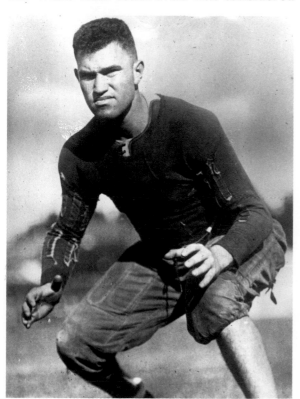

Far left: *John Fox, captain of the 1919 team, played under three different head coaches: Ralph Glaze, Dean Cromwell and Elmer Henderson.*

Left: *Roy (Swede) Evans was the Trojan's best lineman on teams that won 20 of 22 games from 1919-21.*

Right: *Roy Teelen leaps for yardage in USC's 40-7 victory over Occidental in 1920.*

Opposite top right: *Roy Baker (left) defends against a pass during a 41-3 victory over Washington State in 1922.*

Opposite bottom right: *Bill Cook rips off a big gain versus Arizona in a 56-0 victory in 1925.*

USC campus. Only 12,863 turned out for the Coliseum's inaugural game against Pomona, a 23-7 Southern Cal victory, but when the season had ended with a 6-2 record, nearly 260,000 spectators had watched the Trojans in their new home, including a mammoth crowd of 72,000 when California defeated the Trojans 12-0. From that point on, college football in southern California, and Los Angeles in particular, became king and fed off the status the area was developing with its ever-inceasing number of celebrities from an expanding motion picture industry.

Henderson had some great players during those seasons, none finer than lineman Leo Calland and quarterback Chet Dolley. Calland was renowned for his pass-blocking in a time when the forward pass wasn't nearly the weapon it became a half

century later. His talents were useful since Dolley, in the game of that time, had the main task of blocking for the halfback and fullback in the single wing formation which was so popular.

Henderson's last team, in 1924, won 10 of 12 games (back-to-back losses against St. Mary's and old nemesis California) and finished with a 20-7 victory over Missouri in a game dubbed the Christmas Festival. Some 50,000 fans showed up on Christmas Day and saw Hayden Pythian, Wallace Newman, and Henry Lefebvre score touchdowns in a 20-point third quarter spree.

Despite his great success, Henderson's failure to defeat California – he lost all five games against the Bears – and an offhand remark by Notre Dame's Knute Rockne cost him his job. Relations with Cal were never cordial and every loss was like a stab

in the heart. Further, after Notre Dame's Four Horsemen team soundly defeated Stanford in the 1925 Rose Bowl, Rockne quipped, "I'll have to come out and coach USC to show them how to beat a team from the North."

Rockne meant it as a joke but it was taken seriously at USC, where it was considered a not-so-subtle hint that Rockne wanted to become coach. Such a move would have been impossible because Rockne had a contract with Notre Dame, which had no intention of allowing him to escape. Still, USC fired Henderson, and then was totally embarrassed by Rockne's unavailability.

Into the coaching market they went, and the "second choice" became Howard Jones, then head coach at Duke. It was the best "second choice" USC ever made.

2. Kings of the West Coast

There was no denying Howard Jones's football credentials when he came to USC as head coach in 1925. And he went on to achieve Hall of Fame proportions during his 16 seasons at Troy, when he brought Southern California to the pinnacle of West Coast football dominance and the unparalleled national prominence that lasts to this day. He won 121 games that led to five national titles, the most by any USC coach; won or shared six Pacific Coast Conference titles, including five during a six-year period from 1927 through 1932; won a record five Rose Bowls; and produced 23 All-America players.

Jones, who came to USC after one so-so season at Duke, earlier had had two one-year stints at Yale where he became that school's first paid football coach and tutored

some of its legendary players. He added to his experience at Syracuse, Ohio State, and Iowa, where his Hawkeye teams won 42 games in six seasons, including back-to-back Big Ten titles and the school's only unbeaten season in history. At all of those stops, his football style was a plain vanilla single wing attack that operated exclusively from tackle-to-tackle.

Yet, once he arrived at Troy, the perfect playing conditions in California sent a torrent of exotic X's and O's dancing through his mind, and he developed one of the most complex offensive systems in the school's history. He was amusingly considered "the absent-minded professor" whose mind was constantly so preoccupied with new formations and innovations that he was a menace on the highway, often ignoring traffic sig-

Right: *New head coach Howard Jones (right) is greeted by Col. Warren Bovard, an early moving force in the growth of USC football, during 1925 spring practice. Jones won 121 games and five national titles in 16 seasons.*

nals and the traffic around him; lost socks and keys with amazing frequency; forgot appointments and meetings with family members; and even lost his way home.

He had inherited some talented players from Elmer Henderson, including running backs Mort Kaer and Manny Laranetta, and added Morley Drury and Howard Elliott, all of whom still rank among the school's top ground-gainers. They led the first vanguard of Trojan running backs who soon were known as "The Thundering Herd."

Led by Kaer, Jones's first great runner who scored 114 points, including four TDs in one game, they combined to win 11 of 13 games in 1925, the most by any USC team to that time. That running game was helped immensely by the blocking of guard Brice Taylor, a black athlete who became USC's first All-America player. Kaer became the second a year later when USC finally defeated California 27-0 en route to an 8-2 season.

Drury was the key to Southern Cal's attack in 1926 and 1927, and Jones always called him "my favorite player," no small bit of praise considering the number of great stars who performed for his USC teams. "He had aggressiveness, courage, agility, stamina and durability," Jones later said, "all the qualities that any coach sought in a great player."

Drury was a superb athlete who had won high school letters in football, basketball,

water polo, and swimming by the time he entered Southern Cal, at the ripe old age of 21. He became the classic triple threat offensive player, who ran, passed, and kicked, though he preferred playing defense, once noting, "I would rather intercept passes than throw them." In a 13-0 victory over California, he started the game at quarterback and then was at halfback, and finally scored both USC TDs as its fullback. Jones so admired his football instincts that he let him call all the plays.

Drury's greatest season – and greatest frustration – came in 1927, his senior year, when he gained 1163 of his career total 1686 yards. But a 13-13 tie against Stanford cost

Left: *Mainstays of the 1927 line, guards Bert Heiser and Chick Galloway flank center John Fox.*

Above: *Mort Kaer was the first of USC's All-America running backs. Kaer led the Trojans in rushing and scoring in both the 1925 and 1926 seasons.*

Right: *In 1927, Morley Drury was USC's first 1000-yard rusher and was so talented at every phase of the game that coach Howard Jones called him "my favorite player."*

Right: *Halfback Marshall Duffield rips off a gain in a 7-0 win against Stanford that helped Jones's 1929 team to a 9-2 record and USC's second Rose Bowl appearance, where it beat Pitt 47-14.*

the Trojans and Drury what they most longed to achieve – a Rose Bowl bid, through no fault of Drury's, who gained 163 yards and intercepted five passes.

But the frustration ended in 1928 when the Trojans finally achieved their nirvana, winning the Rissman Trophy as national champion for the first time. That team missed a perfect season by a scoreless tie against California in Berkeley in what still is known as the "Mud Bowl." It hadn't rained in the Bay Area for days before the game, yet when the Trojans ran onto the field, they sank ankle-deep into mud. Prime suspects were some Cal rooters and fire hoses which they used to soak the field the night before the game.

There was one other significant victory – a 10-0 win over Stanford, the first of five straight after three unsuccessful tries that settled which West Coast team was the dominant force. It also was a personal triumph for Jones, who had disliked Stanford coach Glenn (Pop) Warner from the time that Warner's Carlisle Indians team, featuring Jim Thorpe, had beaten his Syracuse team and then accused Jones of using illegal tactics. Warner never again beat USC and Jones, and after five straight losses the ignominy was too much for Stanford officials who fired him.

In 1929, the fortunes reversed a bit for Jones. He had his most talented team at

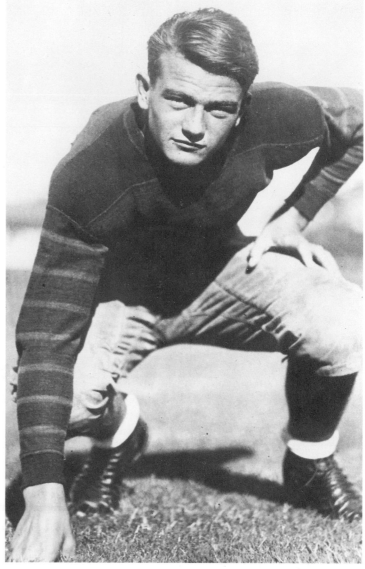

Southern Cal yet missed a national championship because of a 15-7 loss to California and a 13-12 defeat by Notre Dame, to finish with a 9-2 record. This was a star-studded team with such All-Americans as guard Nate Barragar and end Francis Tapaan was well as junior running back Gus Shaver, who many believe was the best all-around back in Trojan history; halfback Ernie Pinckert, who earned his reputation as a fearsome blocker; Russ Saunders, who was selected over his other more talented teammates to pose for the famous bronze statue of Tommy Trojan; and guard Ted Beckett. Their supreme triumph came in crushing unbeaten and untied Pitt, 47-14 in the Rose Bowl.

Their performances drove West Coast writers to unparalleled levels of praise, one of them finally describing the team as "The Thundering Herd," a take-off on a popular Noah Beery western movie of that time. It was a natural tie-in between Southern Cal football and its star-studded team, and Hollywood, home of the nation's newest hero – the movie star. In fact, one of that team's tackles was Ward Bond, later a fine

movie and television actor whose specialty was westerns, as was another would-be USC tackle from a few years earlier, Marion Morrison, better known as John Wayne.

Projected as a starting tackle for the 1926 season, Wayne suffered a pre-season shoulder injury while swimming. This severely hampered his blocking during pre-season drills but he was afraid to tell Jones about the accident, fearing the circumstances would incur his wrath. Sub-par play dropped Wayne to the fifth team and cost him a spot at the team's training table. Thus having to buy his own meals, which he couldn't afford, he dropped out of USC and sought employment as a bit actor in Hollywood. It wasn't too long before he was playing some major roles, and even recruiting USC football players for bit parts in movies that had college football as part of the plot.

Wayne, who appeared in some classic western movies with Bond, never lost his love for USC football. He regularly attended Trojan home games and often traveled to distant parts of the country to

Above left: *All-America guard Nate Barragar keyed a line that helped USC, led by backs Gus Shaver and Ernie Pinckert, roll up a record 492 points in 1929.*

Above: *Future movie great John Wayne, then known as Marion Morrison, was a varsity lineman before lack of funds forced him to leave USC.*

Above: *Hollywood's influence was always present at USC, where several of its players became movie legends. An "All-America" 1934 team included: Front row, from left: Dale Van Sickle (Florida); John Wayne (USC); Nic Foran (Princeton); John Braue (Alabama); Andy Devine (Texas); Monk Saunders (Washington); Bill Bakewell (Washington & Lee). Back row, from left: Norm McLeod (Washington); Pat O'Brien (Marquette); Johnny Mack Brown (Alabama); Charles Starrett (Dartmouth).*

see the team play. And in 1966 when the Trojans opened the season at top-ranked Texas, coach John McKay, a fanatical Wayne movie buff, asked him to talk to the team, and the Duke gave such a rousing performance that the Trojans went out and upset the Longhorns. The players then awarded him their own version of the Oscar – a game ball which became a treasured memento.

USC attracted some of Hollywood's greatest western stars, including not only Wayne and Ward Bond but also gravel-voiced Andy Devine, who often was a regular in the Trojan locker rooms, and Randolph Scott, who sometimes joined the team for pre-game meals. But love of USC football spread to other stars as well. Jones's teams of the late 1920s and early 1930s had a regular following of Hollywood stars such as Oliver Hardy, Gary Cooper, Mary Pickford, Douglas Fairbanks Sr., Harold Lloyd, Norma Talmadge, Richard Dix, Hoot Gibson, and Ronald Colman, many of them becoming such unabashed rooters that they even wrote fan letters to the team. That rooting clientele expanded as the years went on to include William Bendix, whose two most famous roles were protraying slugger Babe Ruth in the movie *The Babe Ruth Story* and Chester A. Riley in the TV series *The Life of Riley*, and Robert Young, who joined Wayne for nearly every USC home game. The adulation continues in the movie community as stars still rub elbows with other fans on sunny fall afternoons at the Coliseum.

After an 8-2 season in 1930, Jones started USC on one of its greatest eras, winning three consecutive national titles in 1931-33 as part of a 27-game unbeaten streak – and

he did it with two different sets of "Thundering Herds." His 1931 team was led by Shaver, Pinckert, Jim Musick, Stan Williamson – one of three Williamsons (Frank and Jack were the others) to play for the Trojans in this era – and Orv Mohler in the backfield, and had two great linemen in Ernie Smith and Aaron Rosenberg. The two were almost opposites because Smith succeeded as much with his desire and courage as he did with ability, while Rosenberg had tremendous physical talent.

This team didn't appear to be going anywhere when it was upset by St. Mary's 13-7 in the opening game of the 1931 season. But the Trojans did not lose again until Stanford beat them 13-7 midway through the 1933 season. Included in the streak was a heroic 16-14 victory over Notre Dame in 1931, and a 13-0 win over the Irish in 1932, as well as a pair of Rose Bowl wins over Tulane and Pitt.

After the Trojans had defeated Tulane, they were awarded the first Knute Rockne Memorial Trophy as national champion, one of several awards in vogue at that time before the wire service polls began deciding national champions. They were declared national champions the following year by both the Dunkel and Williamson rating systems.

Jones's teams from 1929 through 1931 had averaged 38 points a game, but the 1932 team was shorn of its great offensive stars and averaged just 20. So it lived on defense, keyed primarily by Smith and Rosenberg, the latter still considered one of the greatest guards in USC history. The Trojans shut out eight of ten opponents, and allowed only two touchdowns, both on passes, by California and Washington.

Some offensive dash was provided that year by a smallish halfback named Irving (Cotton) Warburton, who was beginning a great three-year career that made him one of USC's top ten rushers to that point. Warburton weighed about 145 pounds when he began his career at USC, and rarely went above 160, though it is doubtful whether Jones ever knew that – if he did, then he violated his rule that a player should be no less than 175 pounds to play on his teams.

Nick Pappas, who succeeded Warburton as one of USC's great tailbacks and idolized him as a USC freshman, recalled standing in the locker room and watching Warburton weigh in prior to a practice. Jones kept track of each players weight before and after every practice.

"The needle hit 158 pounds," Pappas later recalled, "and the manager wrote down 175 pounds."

"'Hey,' I said, 'it was 158 pounds, not 175.' So Warburton looked at me and said, 'How much do you weigh?'

"'I told him 140 pounds, and he said, 'Do you want to play?'

"'Yessir,' I replied.

"'You weigh 175,' he told me, and from that day forward I weighed 175 pounds though I never weighed over 160. And neither did Cotton Warburton," Pappas concluded.

Warburton, who later became an Oscar-winning cinematographer, was equally spectacular on defense, where he played safety. Against Stanford in 1932, he and his defensive backfield mates knocked down 10 passes. Warburton slipped while covering a California receiver and the play resulted in one of the two touchdowns USC allowed that season. With all of his great feats, Warburton never forgot that one play for as long as he lived. In the final game of that perfect season, against Notre Dame, Warburton's punt return set up one touchdown and the defense twice halted the Irish inside the 10-yard line for a 13-0 victory.

In the Rose Bowl against Pitt, the Trojans led 7-0 when Warburton prevented a Pitt runner from scoring with an open field tackle. Then, he broke the game open with two second-half touchdowns and a running exhibition during which Pitt actually tore

Below: USC stops Notre Dame's Steve Banas at the one-yard line to preserve a 16-14 victory in 1931, part of a 27-game unbeaten streak from 1931-33.

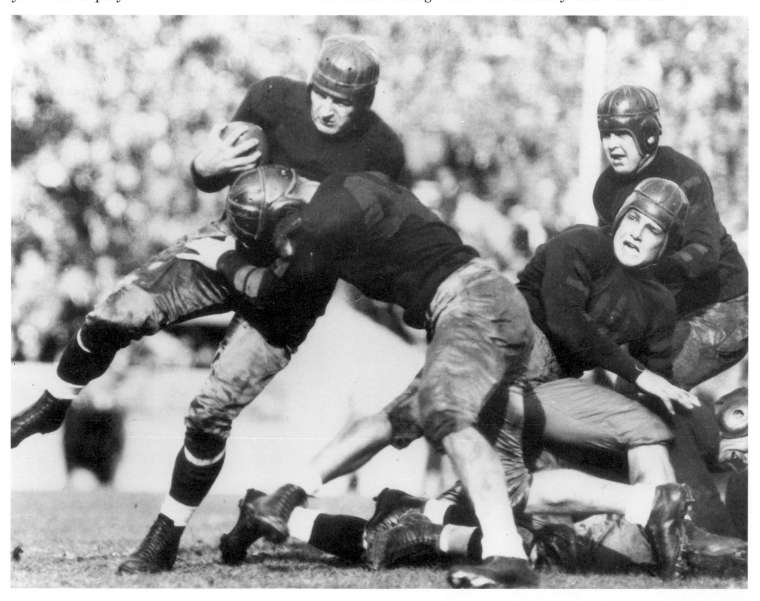

the jersey off his back but still could not stop him.

This first glorious era of Jones's reign at Southern California came to an end after the 1933 season, during which USC lost only one of 12 games and played a scoreless tie against Oregon State that broke their 25-game winning streak. Two weeks later, Stanford's famed "Vow Boys" handed USC its first loss since 1931, and despite a gaudy 10-1-1 record, the Trojans simply packed their gear at season's end and went home. The only post-season bowl at that time was the Rose Bowl, but the loss and tie in conference play cost them the PCC title and a third straight bowl appearance.

Jones's teams at Southern California never again approached the dominance they had enjoyed during his first nine seasons when they were 84-11-3. The closest they came was a 23-game winning streak that began near the end of the 1938 season, lasted through an unbeaten (with two ties) 1939 season, and ended in 1940. The 1938 team posted a 9-2 record, USC's best since 1933, losing to Alabama in the opening game and starting the unbeaten streak after a 7-6 loss to Washington late in the season. This team, as well as the unbeaten 1939 team, was led by Grenny Lansdell, Ambrose Schindler, and Doyle Nave, whose single greatest moment at USC occurred

Opposite top: *Cotton Warburton, USC's leading rusher in 1932-33, gets a "lift" from tackle Al Coughlin.*

Opposite bottom: *USC's 1932 national champions.*

Left: *Grenny Lansdell, who led USC rushers in 1938-39, was one of the Trojans' greatest open field runners.*

when he threw the winning touchdown pass in the final minute of the 1939 Rose Bowl that produced an astounding 7-3 victory over previously unbeaten and un-scored-upon Duke.

Lansdell, a fine all-around offensive back who continually amazed Jones with his great open field running ability and, perhaps more than anything else, his powerful stiff-arm that knocked would-be tacklers flat, still is listed among the Trojans' top rushers and passers. He had a great supporting cast in guard Harry Smith, a two-time All-American and a Hall of Fame inductee, as well as Nave; ends Al Krueger, who caught the winning TD pass against Duke, Bill Fisk and Bob Winslow; tackles Phil Gaspar and Howard Stoecker; Ben Sohn, the "other" guard; and center Ed Dempsey.

Unlike USC's last unbeaten team in 1932, the 1939 group surprised many of its opponents with its power and stamina. Lon Stiner, whose Oregon State team fell 19-7, called it the best team he had ever seen, better than any of Jones's teams during that great nine-year run of the late 1920s and early 1930s. Like their predecessors in 1932, this group played defense as well as it did offense and shut out four opponents that season. They also defeated Notre Dame 20-12 and Washington 9-7. The Trojans faced Tennessee in the Rose Bowl, and for the second straight year met a team that had won every game and had not allowed a point to be scored. But Jones's team polished off its unbeaten season with a 14-0 win, breaking the Vols' 23-game winning streak.

That was Jones's last bit of glory for the men of Troy. His 1940 team won only three games, and soon thereafter he died of a heart attack. But he had set the tone for all who followed.

3. The Cravath and Hill Era

Southern Cal's football bin was all but empty when Howard Jones died suddenly after the 1940 season, and one of his assistants, Sam Barry, became head coach.

He fared even worse, with a 2-6-1 record in 1941. One of those victories was a dramatic 13-7 opening game victory over Oregon State when Doug Essick caught a game-winning six-yard touchdown pass from Ray Woods with just six seconds to play. But it was all downhill after that, and before Barry could solve the situation, World War II intervened, and he was called into the service.

Enter Jeff Cravath. He had been a center and captain of Jones's 1926 team, then served him as an assistant coach for a few years before becoming head coach at the University of Denver. He found his way back to USC as Jones's line coach during the 1939 and 1940 seasons, and when Barry was named head coach, Cravath went to the University of San Francisco as head coach for 1941.

Cravath revitalized USC's football fortunes during his nine seasons, giving its program some consistency with seven straight winning seasons, sandwiched between an opening 5-5-1 year in 1942 and his only losing season in 1950. His teams won four conference titles between 1943 and 1947, and two of four Rose Bowls during that time. His 1944 team was unbeaten.

So much for the numbers. Cravath was a hard-driving coach, much like Jones, who believed that football was of prime importance and demanded a total dedication of body and spirit. He stressed speed and passing, and soon gave his team a much-needed bit of flair by switching to the T-formation offense.

While some of his detractors claimed he was a better line coach than head coach, his program prospered though he never had the talent that Jones had enjoyed during the first nine years of his tenure. Cravath's first great player was Jim Hardy, a native of Los Angeles who had once worked as an usher in the Coliseum and then joined the football team in Jones's last season as a walk-on freshman. Years later he was director of events for the big arena.

Hardy was a starting tailback in Cravath's first season but he switched him to quarterback for his final two years, during

which he set the Pacific Coast Conference ablaze with his passing as well as with his defense (his nine interceptions led the PCC in 1944).

"The move was heaven-sent," Hardy once said, "because I was a much better passer than I was a runner. I didn't have the speed to be a single wing tailback, but I had enough to get by if I got in trouble playing quarterback."

He impressed Cravath in the new coach's very first game, coming off the bench against Tulane with USC trailing 27-0 to score a couple of touchdowns and kick an extra point. He stayed as USC's starting tailback for the rest of the season, and then made the move to quarterback, which paid off with an 8-2 season in 1943 and an 8-0-2 record in 1944, including Rose Bowl victories in both years.

Hardy, of course, didn't do it all himself. In 1942, end Ralph Heywood led the team in pass receptions and punting (he also had been its top punter in 1941) and was its top receiver again in 1943 when he was named to the All-America team.

Of course, all of this was happening in the midst of a world war, and there was a constant ebb and flow of players as some colleges became training grounds for military personnel of all services, building teams with their own players as well as with those who had begun careers at other schools. USC, unlike other schools which were not aligned with ROTC or the Navy V-8 or V-12 programs, had a steady supply of good talent throughout the war years. That is one reason why they beat every college team on their schedule in 1943, and found their two losses coming against San Diego Navy (10-7) and March Field (35-0). Those two service teams had a great array of both

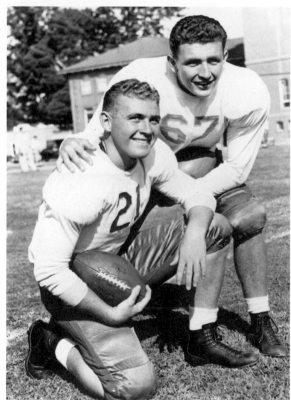

Above: *Coach Jeff Cravath and his 1943 team, which ended an 8-2 season with a 29-0 victory over Washington in the Rose Bowl.*

Left: *Coach Jeff Cravath switched Jim Hardy (left, with brother Don) from tailback to quarterback in his junior season, and he became the Trojans' all-time passing yardage and TD leader.*

college and professional players.

The Trojans also set a record when they shut out their first six opponents. The two service teams broke the perfect record, and then UCLA got 13 points during a season-ending 26-13 Trojan victory. But USC reverted to form and shut out Washington 29-0 in an All-West Coast Rose Bowl that was mandated by wartime travel restrictions (two years earlier, in the aftermath of the Japanese attack on Pearl Harbor and the fear of an invasion by enemy forces, the Rose Bowl was played in Durham, North Carolina between Oregon State and Duke because of a ban against any large assemblages on the West Coast).

Southern Cal was a decided underdog in the 1944 Rose Bowl because of one common opponent – March Field, which had defeated the Trojans 35-0 but had been whomped by the Huskies, 29-0. This was a no-frills Rose Bowl – the famed Tournament of Roses parade consisted of three decorated automobiles, one of which carried the Grand Marshal, Amos Alonzo Stagg, and spoiled a proper celebration for that great pioneer of American football.

But Hardy and the Trojans were immune to the times. Washington bragged that its passing attack, led by Al Akins and Sam Robinson, was all but unstoppable, but Cravath switched his defense from man-for-man to zone coverage a few days before the game and that was the key – three interceptions, and only five completions in 19 attempts. Hardy threw three touchdown passes to George Callanan and Gordon Gray, each of whom scored twice.

Hardy and USC got revenge against San Diego Navy in their unbeaten 1944 season, stunning the heavily favored Sailors 28-21. Hardy had some great running help from Don Doll, who left after that season for two years of military service, but came back to star on two of Cravath's post-war teams. That game also may have been Hardy's finest hour. With the score tied 21-21 and six minutes to play, he went back to punt on

Right: *The hero of USC's 25-0 victory over Tennessee in the 1945 Rose Bowl was 17-year-old Don Burnside, shown here en route to a 35-yard gain that helped USC to its eighth straight bowl win.*

a fourth down at his own 49-yard line, but instead of kicking, and ignoring Cravath's panicked pleas from the sidelines, he danced around until he saw Doll break loose and threw him a 40-yard pass to San Diego's 11-yard line. On the next play, Doll, who with Milford Dreblow amassed 257 yards, ran for the winning TD.

During the war, USC and UCLA also played each other twice each season. USC's two wins over the Uclans in 1943 put them in the Rose Bowl, and in 1944, after an opening 13-13 tie, the Trojans' 40-13 victory clinched the Rose Bowl spot against Tennessee. Hardy always called that final UCLA game the most gratifying of his life.

He scored twice, threw a touchdown pass, and intercepted a couple of UCLA passes, outplaying the Bruins' great All-America back Bob Waterfield, who two years later returned to Los Angeles with the NFL's Rams and led them to some of their finest moments in that very same Coliseum.

In the Rose Bowl, Hardy's final game was marred by a case of the flu and a rash of injuries to his running backs that left 17-year-old Don Burnside as his chief running threat. But that didn't spoil his performance in the Trojans' 25-0 victory over the freshman-laden Vols. Hardy passed for two touchdowns and scored a third – giving him five TD passes and a score in two games. He

Above: *End Ralph Heywood led the Trojans in punting and pass receiving in 1942-43 and was the first USC receiver to amass more than 200 yards in one season. He was a consensus All-American in 1943.*

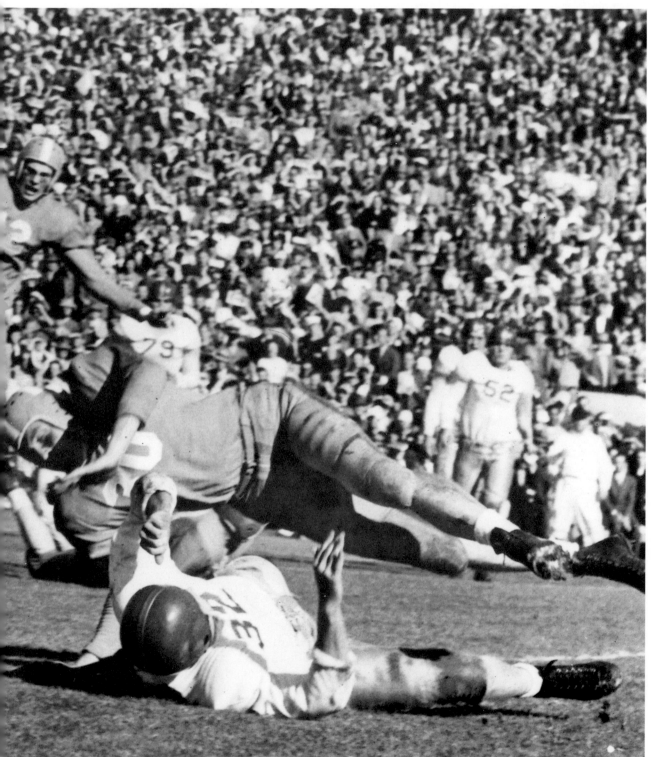

finished with a flourish as his final TD pass went to Doug MacLachlan with six seconds to play.

Cravath brought USC back for Rose Bowl appearances following the 1945 and 1947 seasons, and ran into a buzzsaw both times. First it was Harry Gilmer and a fine Alabama team that defeated them 34-14 as Gilmer rushed for 116 yards and USC was held to an all-time Rose Bowl low of 41 total yards. In 1947, led by two All-Americans, end Paul Cleary and tackle John Ferraro, and paced by Doll, Jim Powers, and Verle Lillywhite, the Trojans were unbeaten (but tied by Rice) until losing to national champion Notre Dame 38-7 in the final game of the season. Their biggest win of the season was a 39-14 victory over California as Doll returned the second half kickoff 95 yards for a touchdown that stretched USC's tight 20-14 halftime lead.

The Rose Bowl was a different – and sadder – story. Michigan coach Fritz Crisler, one of the few coaches who understood that the rules allowed platoon football, overwhelmed Cravath's forces with his constant shuttling of separate offensive and defensive units, and the unbeaten Wolverines hammered USC 49-0. The final score was in no way indicative of the difference between the two teams, but the Trojans simply got worn down from the constant pounding by fresh players – and by All-America back Bob Chappius, who put on a dazzling display by running for 91 yards and passing for 188, and set up or accounted for five Michigan scores.

Cravath's teams posted a cumulative 13-11-5 record during the next three seasons while California's Golden Bears ruled the Pacific Coast Conference – and USC's alumni seethed to the point that with two years still remaining on his contract, Cravath was fired after the 1950 season, his only losing year. Ironically, in his last two games, he faced USC's two most bitter rivals – UCLA and Notre Dame. The Uclans easily won 39-7, but in the final game of his career, his Trojans upset Notre Dame 9-7 after Jim Sears, whose fumble had led to the Irish touchdown, returned a kick 44 yards for USC's only score.

Cravath's successor was Jess Hill, who once had set an IC4A broad jump record and had been a fine running back for the Trojans in the late 1920s; had hit a home run on his first pitch as a professional player, for Hollywood in the old Pacific Coast League; and who had once romped with Babe Ruth during New York Yankee exhibition games in the early 1930s while embarking on a major league career that took him also to the Washington Senators and the Philadelphia Athletics.

Hill had returned to USC in 1946 as assistant track coach under Dean Cromwell, and succeeded him in 1949. When he was named football coach, he brought an even-keel personality to USC's football program, much-needed some claimed, because Cravath had lived in the eye of a storm at times with his players as well as with some of the school's fans and alumni. Winning was important to Hill, but not all-consuming, at least for a time. It was more important that his team was fully prepared and gave an all-out effort; if it won, that was the result of hard work, but a loss didn't diminish the hard work or effort. His philosophy and work ethic were successful enough to produce 45 wins over six seasons, a Pacific Coast Conference title in 1952, and two Rose Bowl appearances, including the PCC's first victory over the Big Ten, 7-0 against Wisconsin in 1953.

That win climaxed his best season, during which his team was unbeaten until losing its final regular game, 9-0 against Notre Dame. But it was in his first year as head coach, 1951, that he recorded what he always considered his most significant victory when the Trojans trailed top-ranked California 14-0 at Berkeley and won 21-14, breaking Cal's 38-game regular-season winning streak.

Frank Gifford, who had been used pri-

Below: *Tackle John Ferraro was a 19-year-old All-America tackle in 1944, and after military service, twice made the All-PCC team and was a consensus All-American again in 1947.*

Left: *Halfback Frank Gifford (16), later an NFL Hall of Fame player with the New York Giants, gave New Yorkers a preview of coming attractions as a single wing tailback during a game at Yankee Stadium against Army in 1951.*

Left: *Gifford was chased out of his passing pocket and then dodged and twisted his way through much of Army's defense for a big gain. Gifford, who first made his mark on defense, was most effective as a tailback at USC.*

marily as a defensive back by Cravath but had become the focal point in a new, multi-dimensional T and single wing offense that Hill installed, was the star of the game. He got USC's first TD on a 69-yard run, and then threw a halfback option pass to Dean

Schneider for the tie-maker. Gifford's punting sealed California in its own end of the field late in the fourth quarter, and with less than five minutes to play, the Trojans began their last drive. Gifford made a key first down with inches to spare at Cal's 12-

Right: *Phil Debovsky (77), Mike Henry (78, who later played Tarzan in the movies), and Lyle Clark (52) carry coach Jess Hill off the field after a 28-20 victory over Notre Dame to end the 1956 season. Hill then became athletic director.*

yard line, and three plays later Leon Sellers scored the winning TD and Gifford kicked the final point.

Gifford and Jim Sears were the stars of Hill's early teams, but they took some divergent paths to gain their stardom. Sears was the acknowledged star as a sophomore, Gifford a lowly substitute who had come from Bakersfield, California, and finally won himself a job as a defensive back under Cravath after he came off the bench to replace an injured player and came up with three interceptions. He stayed on defense during two seasons because he was ill-suited to play in Cravath's T offense. But when Hill came up with his multiple offense concept, Gifford played every offensive backfield position, and did the punting and placekicking. He was a marvelous tailback in Hill's single wing, and led the Trojans with 841 yards and added another 303 from passing.

Sears, just 5' 11" and 175 pounds, had won Cravath's confidence because he was a gutsy player who also performed in key situations. After he lost the key backfield role to Gifford in 1951, he honed himself into an all-around player who could run and throw with equal facility, return kickoffs and punts, and play safety on defense. He became USC's big gun in their PCC championship season of 1952. Sears was most effective when he was the tailback in Hill's single wing offense. But he also was a better passer than Gifford and, playing either as the T formation quarterback or the tailback, had nine TD passes among his 53 completions during the 1952 season.

In what was supposed to be his finest day – the Rose Bowl game against Big Ten champion Wisconsin – Sears was hurt early in the first quarter and did not play again. Instead, Rudy Bukich came off the bench and led the Trojans to a 7-0 victory, the first time a Pacific Coast Conference team had defeated the Big Ten champion since the exclusive Rose Bowl arrangement started in the late 1940s.

The 1952 season was the highlight of Hill's head coaching tenure at USC, though in 1954 the 8-3 Trojans, second to the Uclans, made it back to the Rose Bowl because PCC champions could not have repeat appearances. They lost to Ohio State, 20-7. The previous season, 1953, the Trojans were 6-3-1, losing their final two games to UCLA and Notre Dame, but staged one of the great finishes in USC history a week before the UCLA game to come away with a 23-20 victory over Stanford on Sam Tsagalakis's 38-yard field goal with 13 seconds to play.

The 1955 team turned in a 6-4 record, including a momentous 42-20 victory over Notre Dame in the season's final game. New stars were backs Aramis Dandoy, Jon Arnett, and C.R. Roberts, as well as end Leon Clarke. Arnett could have been one of the greatest backs in Southern Cal history had not his career been cut short by an illegal payment scandal. He was a graceful, fluid runner who seemed to be guided away from opposing tacklers by radar. He led the Trojans in rushing as a sophomore with 601 yards in 1954, despite missing time with an ankle injury, and again as a junior with 672 yards.

This was not yet the age of the USC tailback, where that featured player got the ball 35 or 40 times a game. Instead, Arnett shared the running with Roberts, a burly fullback and the first black starting player at USC since lineman Brice Taylor in 1925. Roberts played in 1955 and 1956, and finished with 1309 career yards, including 251 yards against Texas in just over 12 minutes of play as the Trojans rolled to a 44-20 victory to open the 1956 season. He had three scoring runs of over 45 yards in that game. He had another explosive game in a 35-7 victory over Washington.

How great the Arnett-Roberts tandem might have been over a full college career will never be known, because they were shorn of eligibility – Arnett lost the second half of the 1956 season, during which he was the leading candidate for the Heisman Trophy, and Roberts lost all of 1957 – for accepting illegal payments as part of a scandal that rocked the entire PCC, costing players from many PCC schools, including 11 from USC, eligibility and games. It eventually led to the dissolution of the conference and a total restructuring of West Coast football.

Hill always professed ignorance of the violations, but as head coach, it was his responsibility to keep track of such matters in his program. He resigned after the 1956 season and became athletic director.

Left: *Halfback Jon Arnett, USC's leading rusher in 1954 and 1955, was so agile that if he was propelled into the air after being hit, he could land on his feet in a crouch, and take off again. He might have won the Heisman Trophy as a senior had he not been forced to forfeit half his season because of rules violations.*

4. McKay's Student Body Right and Left

Below: *John McKay won the first of his four national championships in 1962 with a quarterback triumvirate of, from left, Craig Fertig, Pete Beathard, and Bill Nelsen. Beathard was the starter because, in the age of limited substitution, he also could play defensive back.*

Great running backs had been the forte of USC football since the days of Howard Jones, but John McKay raised the genre to unheard-of levels during his tenure as Trojan head coach from 1960 to 1975. During that time, two Heisman Trophy winners – Mike Garrett and O.J. Simpson – and such stars as Willie Brown, Clarence Davis, and Anthony Davis blazed a smoking trail across the turf at the Los Angeles Coliseum, where USC's explosive offense was dubbed "student body right and student body left."

It wasn't all running power, because

McKay also had fine quarterbacks such as Pete Beathard, Craig Fertig, Steve Sogge, Jim Jones, Mike Rae, and probably his best, Pat Haden. All of them, combined with an array of fine players at other positions, enabled McKay and the Trojans to win 127 of 175 games, four national championships, eight Rose Bowl appearances and an 18-3 dominance over bitter rivals UCLA and Notre Dame.

McKay had succeeded Don Clark as head coach. Clark, who had been captain of Jeff Cravath's teams just a decade before, had replaced Jess Hill in 1957, and faced an im-

possible task of running a football program that was torn asunder in the wake of the eligibility scandals and relegated to second-class citizen status throughout the university. There were no resources for upgrading facilities or resources and even if there had been, the penalties assessed against the Trojans included a prohibition against football scholarships, thereby depriving Clark of young, talented players to replace 11 lettermen lost by graduation and eight others ruled ineligible for 1957.

Clark won just one game in his first season but, with the help of new president Dr. Norman Topping who rescued USC football from limbo, he turned the program around and had an 8-2 record in his third and final year. He was offered a five-year contract to continue as head coach, but those three tough seasons had burned out his intensity for the game, and he resigned.

Enter McKay, who had been Clark's backfield coach, and before that had been an assistant coach at the University of Oregon since his graduation in 1949 where he and quarterback Norm Van Brocklin had helped lead the Ducks to the co-championship of the Pacific Coast Conference. Football was like a vacation for McKay, because he had been raised in the coal mining community of Shinniston, West Virginia, where he also had worked for a year as a coal miner. World War II helped him to escape that life, because he spent four years in the Air Force where he saw plenty of combat as a tail gunner in a heavy bomber; he then used his G.I. Bill benefits for a college education and football career, for a year at Purdue, and then at Oregon.

McKay had to call on the lessons that he learned during the hardship of his youth in Appalachia when USC had losing records during his first two seasons. But in 1962, the team did a complete turnaround and won the national championship with an 11-0 record, including a 42-37 victory over Wisconsin in one of the greatest Rose Bowl games ever played.

The success of the 1962 team was born the previous year when McKay swallowed a losing season and relied heavily on his sophomores, Brown, Beathard, and All-America end Hal Bedsole, who had come to USC as a quarterback and requested a position change to end when he saw the QB talent ahead of him. Beathard moved ahead of veteran Bill Nelsen at quarterback because he had better physical skills and greater mobility. But whenever Beathard ran into trouble, McKay called on Nelsen's leadership and experience to come up with a victory.

That team was more balanced in running and passing than later teams featuring

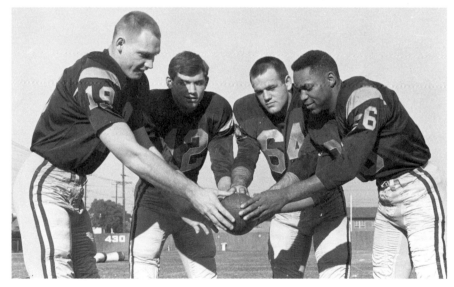

Garrett, Simpson, and Davis, and was certainly not as talented. In fact, it was not a big team by later USC standards, and depended a great deal on its defense to get through tough moments, allowing just 55 points during 10 regular season games. It flashed into the national consciousness with an opening 14-7 upset victory over Duke in a nationally televised game and just rolled onward, finally coming down to the two final games, against UCLA and Notre Dame. The Bruins led 3-0 with five minutes to play, but Brown made a great catch of a Beathard pass for a touchdown and the Trojans went on to a 14-3 victory. Against Notre Dame, Beathard didn't complete a pass to Bedsole but he got plenty of

Top: *Coach John McKay celebrated the Trojans' first undefeated season in 30 years in 1962 by leading a pep rally at the Coliseum.*

Above: *Two All-Americans, end Hal Bedsole (19) and guard Damon Bame (64), and QB Pete Beathard (12) and back Willie Brown, were keystones of the 1962 national champion team.*

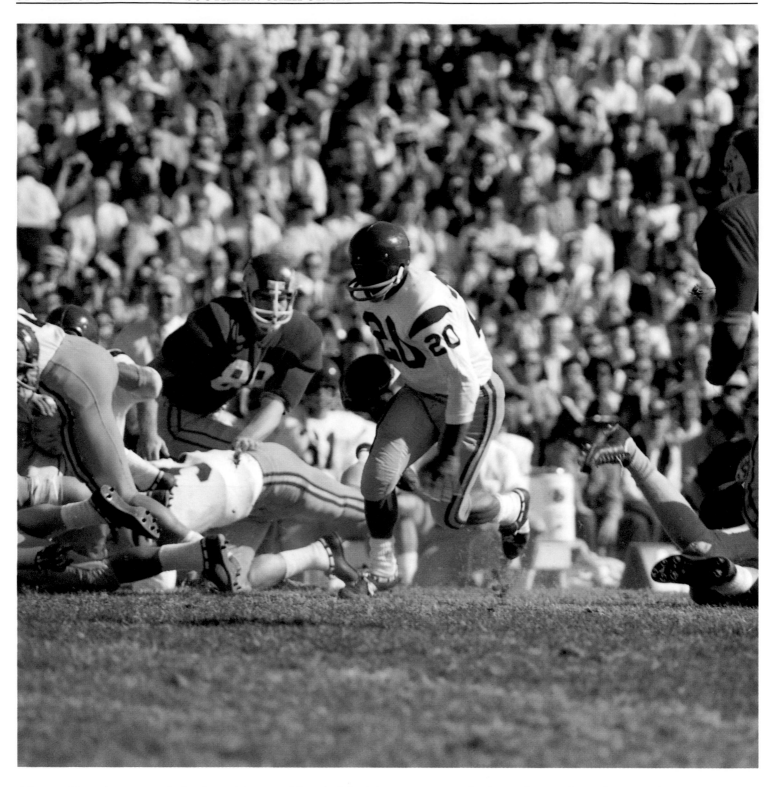

Above: *Running back Mike Garrett's speed and power allowed McKay to develop his I-formation offense. Garrett became the first of the Trojans' great tailbacks during this era. Though just 5′9″ and 185 pounds, he produced 3221 rushing yards in three years.*

help from Brown, blended in his own running, and came away with a 25-0 victory. In the Rose Bowl, USC roared to a 35-14 lead after three quarters and had to hold off a furious Wisconsin 23-point fourth quarter for the eventual victory, carving out USC's first perfect season since 1932 and its first national championship since 1933.

When McKay landed Garrett from Roosevelt High School in L.A. and saw his great running ability, he shifted USC's primary offense to the I formation, where his fullback and tailback, or "Z" back in his terminology, were lined up behind the quarterback and able to break quickly to the right or left. But he maintained a well-

balanced attack with a good passing game so that opposing teams could not set defenses to stop only the run. Woody Hayes, when he coached at Ohio State and had to solve those problems in a couple of Rose Bowl games, said that no team integrated its running and passing better than McKay's teams – even with great running backs like Garrett, Simpson, and Davis.

Garrett was not very big, at 5′ 9″ and only 180 pounds, but he was very quick and durable. He turned so quickly in midstride, without losing speed, that often he fooled his own blockers and ran past them. He also was a "test tube baby" of sorts for McKay, who began to perfect his I-formation offense during Garrett's years, and later allowed his other tailbacks more freedom to choose their holes as they saw a play developing.

But Garrett did well enough in this system to become only the second West Coast player ever to win the Heisman Trophy – Terry Baker of Oregon State had done it in 1962 – with a great 1965 season. He was the second Trojan runner to surpass 1000 yards with 1440, almost half of his career total of 3221 yards. Though he led the Trojans in rushing during each of his three varsity seasons (and he also played defensive back in 1963 when there was no free substitution in college football), USC's 1965 team was considered the least talented of the three on which he played. Yet that team probably worked harder than the others, and Garrett was the ultimate beneficiary.

McKay's 1966 team, with Don McCall at tailback, Troy Winslow at quarterback, and Rod Sherman the only talented wide receiver, had its highlight in the very first game – a stunning 10-6 victory over projected national champion Texas (for which John Wayne got his game ball) in Austin, Texas. USC got the ball at its two-yard line with eight minutes to play and never relinquished it again, making a crucial fourth-and-one play. That team also hit an all-time low with a 51-0 loss to Notre Dame, USC's worst defeat ever.

Still, the team won the AAWU (Athletic Association of Western Universities, successor to the troubled PCC) title but lost 14-13 to Purdue in the Rose Bowl, only because McKay ordered the team to try for a two-point conversion after it had scored

its second touchdown on McCall's run with two and a half minutes to play. Purdue's defensive back George Catavolos broke up Winslow's pass to Jim Lawrence. "We had no intention of playing for a tie," McKay said.

After that, there were more smiles than frowns at USC because the next season, 1967, McKay unveiled a tailback named Orenthal James Simpson, who had set junior college rushing and scoring records during two seasons at the City College of San Francisco, despite being used often as a wide receiver. At USC, his biggest catch was a Heisman Trophy.

Simpson was a sturdy 205 pounds over a 6' 1" frame and had world class speed (he once set a world-record 38.6 seconds as a member of USC's 440-yard relay team), yet as incredible as it may seem now, some

Left: *Mike Garrett, right, poses for a photo with his mother and coach John McKay after winning the 1965 Heisman Trophy. The first USC player to receive the award, he gained a then-record 1440 yards during the 1965 season. His biggest disappointment was never having the chance to play in a Rose Bowl.*

Left: *O. J. Simpson – The Juice – was college football's pre-eminent running back during his two All-America seasons in 1967-68. The most famous of all Trojan tailbacks, he won the Heisman Trophy following the 1968 season after gaining a record-setting 1880 yards.*

questioned whether he could play for USC. Would his great open-field running style meld with McKay's offense? Could he take the pounding required of a USC tailback? How serious was his reputation for fumbling the ball? Could he run out of McKay's I formation?

McKay said later, "We had to make him something he had never been – a running back. He had to rebuild his life completely and it was tough for him early on because he fumbled too much when he ran inside."

McKay decided to get some quick answers, and a few days after spring practice began, he ordered Simpson's number called for seven straight plays. When it seemed he got faster and stronger with every carry, the worries disappeared and McKay then resorted to an old military adage: When you have a big gun, keep firing it. And he did, an average of 32 times a game – 674 times in all - during Simpson's two seasons at USC, during which he gained 3423 yards, including an NCAA-record 1880 in 1968.

Simpson ran with a distinct style and grace as befits a thoroughbred athlete. He never seemed to give tacklers a solid shot at him, though his favorite play was called "22 Blast" or "23 Blast" (depending on whether it was run to the right or left of the center) and it was nothing more than the T formation's most basic play – a "quick-opener" or straight ahead play where linemen simply wedged open a bit of daylight and he shot through.

He could also make holes when there were none, explode into open areas, and be on his way, sidestepping here, cutting back there, changing pace over there – but always moving downfield, always gaining ground. Sometimes he abandoned the play and popped to either side where an anxious defense may have overcommitted too quickly and left a natural opening. When the Trojans ran their "student body series," wide runs to either side, Simpson was at his most dangerous, because he either swept wide or flashed through a natural opening and got into the secondary. McKay had been more restrictive with Garrett but realized later that Mike could have been even more productive if he was allowed to "run to daylight," and gave Simpson that latitude. In his senior year, he scored 23 of the Trojans' 24 rushing touchdowns, and many still wonder what total numbers he might have rung up had McKay also involved him as a pass receiver out of the backfield.

He gained instant national attention with a 164-yard performance against Texas in the second game of the 1967 season, during which he carried the ball 30 times and outrushed the entire Texas team. "I doubt whether there is a back with more ability than Simpson in the country," Texas coach Darrell Royal said afterwards.

He quickly followed that with four consecutive 100-plus-yard games, including 190 against Michigan and 169 against Notre Dame when the Trojans won at South Bend for the first time since 1939. Simpson shared honors that day with linebacker Adrian Young, who intercepted Irish quarterback Terry Hanratty three times to blunt Notre Dame's offense before The Juice finally got rolling in the fourth quarter with a tie-breaking 36-yard TD run en route to a 24-7 victory. While McKay always saw that victory as the turning point of the championship season, Simpson's most significant play was a 64-yard touchdown run against UCLA that nailed down a Rose Bowl berth and the national championship – McKay's second – in one fell swoop.

There was more to USC that season than Simpson, including two fine quarterbacks in Toby Page and Steve Sogge; a swift wide receiver named Earl McCullough; an All-America tackle, Ron Yary, who later won the Outland Trophy as best college lineman; and three fine defensive players, Young, end Tim Rossovich, and defensive back Mike Battle. They helped the Trojans cap their once-beaten season (a 3-0 loss to Oregon State in the rain, though Simpson had 188 yards) with a 14-3 win over Indiana in the Rose Bowl, as O.J. scored both touch-

Above: *O. J. Simpson flashed onto the scene in 1967 with a record-breaking 1543 yards and led the Trojans to the national championship.*

Right: *Quarterback Steve Sogge had the easiest job in the world – handing the ball to O. J. Simpson. But he also finished among the top 10 passers in USC history.*

downs in a 128-yard day and was named the game's MVP.

In 1968, Simpson was a marked man, by opposing defenses who spent so much of their efforts to stop him, and by the public which expected great performances every week. He was very even-handed in this regard – he whipped the opposition and delighted the fans, while at the same time bearing some tremendous physical punishment that began on opening day with 367 yards – 236 rushing – against Minnesota. He carried the ball 39 times for 189 yards despite a badly bruised left thigh that almost benched him in the next game against Northwestern; and then outgained the entire University of Miami offense with 38 carries for 163 yards.

Stanford showed up with "Squeeze O.J." and "O.J. Who?" painted on their helmets, and despite his leg miseries, he answered both questions with 47 carries, 220 yards, and three touchdown runs in USC's 27-24 victory. Against Washington, he gained 172 yards, prompting Huskies coach Jim Owens to note: "We knew Simpson would be coming but there was nothing we could do about it."

The Trojans were in a tough battle against unbeaten Oregon State for the Pacific Eight (the new conference name) title and another Rose Bowl berth until Simpson's 40-yard touchdown run capped a 17-7 victory. Once again, he was more "horse" than "juice," because for the second time that year (previously against Stanford) he carried the ball a record-tying 47 times, this time for 238 yards, including 138 in the last quarter.

The Trojans were the nation's top-ranked team until their final game against Notre Dame at the Coliseum, when the Irish held Simpson to just 55 yards, 23 in the first half en route to a 21-7 lead. McKay relied more on his passing to rally for a 21-21 tie in the second half, but that cost the Trojans their top ranking, and Ohio State finished off any thoughts of a second straight national championship with a 27-17 victory in the Rose Bowl that secured the title for the Buckeyes. USC grabbed a 10-0 lead, helped by Simpson's last great play for them – an 80-yard touchdown run in the second quarter when he swept left and then cut back behind nearly every Ohio State defensive player. Though he lost a pair of fumbles, that run was part of a 276-yard total offense day, including 171 rushing.

Southern Cal had another unbeaten season in 1969, with only a 14-14 tie against Notre Dame marring a perfect record, but could finish no higher than third, even with a 10-3 victory over Michigan in the Rose Bowl. The specialty this time was gut-

wrenching victories achieved by a defense nicknamed "The Wild Bunch," featuring ends Jimmy Gunn and Charley Weaver and tackles Al Cowlings and Tody Smith, and a sophomore quarterback named Jimmy Jones, who came from Pennsylvania to establish himself as a record-breaking passer in southern California. Playing in 1969-71, he became the school's all-time total offense leader with 4501 yards, with 4092 yards and 30 touchdowns from pass-

Top: *Simpson's power and world class speed led to 3423 career rushing yards.*

Above: *All-America tackle Ron Yary won the 1968 Outland Trophy, awarded to the nation's best college lineman.*

Right: *The "Wild Bunch" defense of 1969, from left: Al Cowlings, Jimmy Gunn, Willard Scott, Charles Weaver, and Tody Smith.*

Below: *Quarterback Jimmy Jones, renowned for his "hot" passing hand, teamed with tailback Clarence Davis for an undefeated season in 1969.*

ing. He got 13 in 1969 to break the school record while pulling out some exciting last-minute victories.

The newest in the honorable line of the USC tailback was Clarence Davis, who had broken Simpson's junior college rushing records. He was not as big nor as fast as The Juice, but he was good enough to lead the Trojan rushers in each of his two varsity seasons, despite missing part of his last year with injuries.

Even with Jones's heroics, the Wild Bunch, and Davis's running, the Trojans were in a funk until 1972 when they picked up their third national title with the best record in the school's history – 12-0, including a mighty 42-17 win over Ohio State in the Rose Bowl. Many still believe that this was the finest Southern Cal team of all time – those who didn't see Jones's 1932 team were willing to debate the point – because it not only didn't lose a game, but it also overwhelmed opponents with quarterback Mike Rae, tailbacks Anthony Davis and Rod McNeil, fullback Sam (Bam) Cunningham, and receivers Lynn Swann, J.J. McKay, and Charley Young. They began with a 31-10 demolition of Arkansas in the first game, and finished as the second-highest-scoring Trojan team ever with 467 points, an average of 39 points a game.

There was sharp contrast in the USC backfield. McNeil was a blithe spirit tailback, and Cunningham was a big fullback whose speed and elusiveness enabled him to play tailback the previous year. But he gained fame with his "up and over" technique of hurdling goal line defenses and flying into the end zone. When he wasn't catching passes, Swann was a fearsome punt returner, with one of 92 yards for a TD in a 51-6 victory over Michigan State.

But the star of the 1972 team was sophomore tailback Anthony Davis, who came to Southern Cal from San Fernando High School with a great reputation. He developed more slowly than expected and didn't start until the eighth game of the year (McNeil started the first seven). Still, he built himself a Simpson-like reputation by scoring twice in a 55-20 win over Illinois; added a pair of TDs against Stanford; gained 178 yards in 23 carries against UCLA, including a 23-yard touchdown run; and had his biggest day of all with six touchdowns in a 45-23 win over Notre Dame. He broke five school records that afternoon as he accounted for 368 total yards, including 99 from rushing and a pair of kickoff returns of 97 on the opening kick-

off, and 96 in the third quarter that broke open a close game since Notre Dame had just scored and closed to within two points at 25-23.

Their great performance in the Rose Bowl moved Ohio State coach Woody Hayes to call USC "the best college team I have ever seen." Cunningham got a bowl-record four TDs, Davis ran for 157 yards, and Rae passed for 229 yards, with six receptions going to Swann.

Davis stayed around to produce one last national title for McKay, in 1974, when the Trojans were 10-1-1. He had racked up a 1000-yard season in 1973 when the Trojans, with five All-America players, turned in a 9-2-1 record (the losses were to Notre Dame and Ohio State in the Rose Bowl) even though McKay had to replace 19 of 22 starters. But in 1974, Davis had his best season at USC with 1421 rushing yards, running his career total to 3724 yards. He finished with 52 career touchdowns and an incredible six kickoff-return touchdowns. "My style was to scratch and claw for every yard," Davis said. "And if two yards were

Left: *Anthony Davis continued the tradition of great USC tailbacks from 1972-74. He racked up 3724 career yards, and ranks as the third best rusher in USC history.*

Above: *Fullback Sam (Bam) Cunningham makes one of his patented dives into the end zone for one of his four touchdowns in the 1973 Rose Bowl that led to a 42-17 victory over Ohio State. The win capped a perfect season and McKay's third national championship.*

there, I'd take them and try for a couple more."

McKay paired Davis with a young back named Ricky Bell in 1973 and 1974, and Bell later became his successor at tailback in 1975 and 1976 and finished his career among the top five rushers in USC history. He was primarily a blocker while working with Davis, and he did a passable job.

Of course, Davis didn't do his best work by himself, and in 1974, McKay had a smallish, blond quarterback named Pat Haden, who the previous year had passed for more than 1800 yards. Haden ran McKay's offense flawlessly – he didn't have to do too much passing or complex thinking, even though he became a Rhodes Scholar, with Davis running the ball so well – and the Trojans scored 363 points and never really were pushed, except in their only two losses. Though they had an offensive line that featured All-Americans Bill Bain at guard and tackle Marvin Powell, the Trojans were even stronger on defense with such players as end Gary Jeter, linebacker Richard Wood, and defensive backs Marvin Cobb and Charles Phillips.

Ironically, Haden had the worst game of his career when the Trojans opened at Arkansas in 1974, and injuries to every offensive lineman forced McKay to cancel all heavy contact work the week prior to the game. So the Trojans simply weren't prepared to play – and it showed. Three interceptions (Haden didn't complete a pass until the third quarter and finished with just six completions in 18 attempts) helped produce all the Arkansas points in a 22-7 loss.

The following week against Pitt featured a long-awaited matchup between A.D.

West and T.D. East – Anthony Davis against Tony Dorsett – and A.D. won easily as he outgained Dorsett 149-59 in a 16-7 victory. Defense took over the following week as Phillips picked off a pair of fumbles in mid-air against Iowa and turned them into touchdowns while Davis ran 80 yards for another score in a 45-7 victory. The Trojans were 6-1 when quarterback Steve Bartkowski and the California Golden Bears came to the Coliseum, and despite a pair of 119-yard rushing days from Davis and his sub, Allen Carter, all USC could get was a 15-15 tie when Haden passed for a crucial two-point PAT to end Jim O'Bradovich.

There were no other worries that season, which was punctuated by a tremendous 55-24 victory over Notre Dame after USC had fallen behind 24-6 at halftime. Davis scored four TDs, giving him 11 for his career against the Irish, and Haden had four TD passes for a school season record of 31.

All that remained was an 18-17 victory over Ohio State in the Rose Bowl, the third straight year the two teams had faced each other. USC was fourth-ranked going into the game and the Buckeyes ranked second, but when the game ended with Haden's 38-yard TD pass to J.J. McKay with 2:03 to play, the Trojans were national champions for the fourth time under McKay.

McKay stayed one last season at USC, 1975, and then left to begin an impossible task – starting an expansion franchise at Tampa Bay in the National Football League. He never achieved the success in the NFL that he enjoyed at USC, but he had the satisfaction of knowing that for all time, the USC tailback running student body right and left would be his greatest legacy.

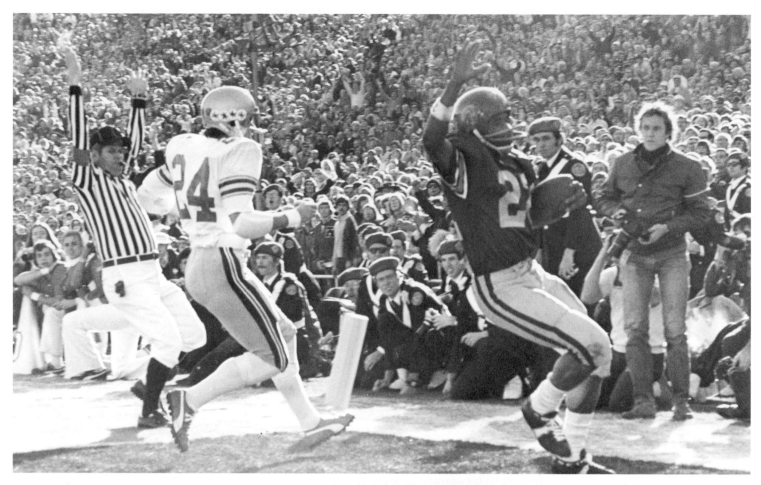

Above: *Another key member of the national champion 1972 team was receiver Lynn Swann. All-America in 1973, he went on to a memorable pro career with the Pittsburgh Steelers.*

Left: *Quarterback Pat Haden (10) and coach John McKay. Haden led USC to a No. 1 ranking in 1974.*

5. The Great Tailbacks Era (Part II)

Below: *Quarterback Vince Evans blossomed under new coach John Robinson in 1976, and, helped by the running of tailback Ricky Bell, led the Trojans to 11 victories and a Rose Bowl victory over Michigan.*

John Robinson had left John McKay's staff to join the Oakland Raiders of the NFL in 1975 at the behest of his childhood friend John Madden, then the Raiders' head coach. Madden placed great reliance on his assistant coaches because his own expertise was very limited and he needed talented assistants to do all of the nuts and bolts football work while he served as a conduit for weekly marching orders from team major domo Al Davis.

Robinson jumped at the opportunity because it appeared at the time that McKay would be a fixture at USC for years to come, and this was a good opportunity for him to gain a new dimension of football experience, hopefully leading to a head coaching job in the NFL, or certainly at the major college level. When McKay announced that he was leaving USC to take over control of the new Tampa Bay Buccaneers franchise of the NFL in 1976, Robinson was offered the job.

Robinson was a perfect choice to succeed McKay because he knew the way that USC operated its program and was still familiar with much of its talent. He also had a perfect personality to handle the peculiarities of college football, where recruiting young players and dealing with college administrators were often as important as calling the correct pass play.

Robinson still liked college football and he had not been in the NFL long enough to have been saturated with its style of play. His playbook still featured Student Body Right and Left, and he worshipped at the feet of the USC tailback. During his seven seasons with the Trojans, he had two Heisman Trophy winners, Charles White and Marcus Allen, before returning to pro football with the Los Angeles Rams.

That kind of talent enabled him to win national championships in 1976, his first season back at Troy, and two years later in 1978; to win three Rose Bowls; and to produce a 97-14-2 record that also included an unbeaten season in 1979 where only a 21-21 tie against Stanford cost his team the national championship.

Having tailback Ricky Bell on hand wasn't a bad way to begin his head coaching career at USC. Bell, at 6′ 1″ and 212 pounds, had been paired with Anthony Davis as a fullback, and then became the tailback in 1976. He was one of the strongest backs ever to play at USC, and carved out 3689 rushing yards, coming within 35 yards of Davis's career record. He was bigger and stronger than most USC tailbacks, bigger even than some of the fullbacks of the McKay era, and almost as shifty as Mike Garrett. He wasn't as highly touted as Garrett, Simpson, or Davis, and this lack of notoriety allowed him to develop without

Left: *Tailback Ricky Bell, a former fullback, ranks fourth among USC's career rushers with 3689 yards from 1973-76.*

Below: *John Robinson worked for a year for his childhood buddy John Madden on the Oakland Raiders staff before succeeding John McKay as USC head coach in 1976.*

the pressure of being an immediate star. It may also have cost him a Heisman Trophy. The fact that he was a starter on a so-so (for USC) team in McKay's last season also hurt his cause but he thrived in his senior year under Robinson, who has always paid tribute to Bell's intensity and determination.

In 1976 Bell scored 14 touchdowns, but he only got one when the Robinson era started on a flat note as Missouri spoiled his homecoming party with a 46-25 victory. The loss is still difficult to understand, considering that USC's offense rolled up 452 yards, 22 first downs and got 172 yards from Bell. But Missouri, which gained 486 yards, used three turnovers for three touchdowns.

Threatening to do a Jekyll-and-Hyde routine, the Trojans turned around the following week and smothered Oregon 53-0 as Bell scored four touchdowns, the first on a 63-yard run, and gained 193 yards in 32 runs. Quarterback Vince Evans added his own dimension with a 13-of-16 day in a 31-13 victory over Purdue, the best performance ever by a USC quarterback. As if that wasn't good enough, Evans succumbed to the flu during the following week's game against Iowa, and Rob Hertel came on and completed a 55-0 rout. Bell gained 119 yards, and the Trojan fans got a glimpse of the future when his understudy, freshman

Above: *Heisman Trophy winner Charles White was the first tailback to gain over 2000 yards, with 2050 in 1979.*

game playing fullback when injuries wiped out all three men at that position.

"This was his last chance before a national TV audience to go out in a blaze of glory, yet he switched and played fullback and played with enthusiasm," Robinson said later. The Trojans had a 14-0 lead after three quarters primarily because the defense came up with four turnovers when the Irish were within scoring distance.

Bell's career at USC really ended with that game, because in the first series of the Rose Bowl against Michigan he was knocked out and never returned to play. Instead, White came on and gained 114 yards in 32 carries as the Trojans won the game 14-6 against a Wolverines team that was ranked fifth nationally on defense and first in total offense. Michigan quickly moved to a 6-0 lead but USC came right back to score, and got the clincher in the fourth quarter on White's seven-yard touchdown run.

While both national wire services acclaimed Pitt as national champion and USC as No. 2, the renowned Dunkel system, which figures its national champions on a power rating index, said the Trojans were No. 1. USC didn't disagree.

Two years later, Southern Cal was again acclaimed national champion by the nation's football coaches, who vote in the poll conducted by United Press International, after USC won 12 of 13 games, losing only to Arizona State 20-7. White was the big star with 1859 rushing yards, the third highest individual season total in USC history, but this time he also had some added help from quarterback Paul McDonald, a left-hander who equalled Rob Hertel's all-time season TD pass mark of 19, and had two fine receivers in Kevin Williams and Calvin Sweeney. Perhaps the unsung offensive player on that team was fullback Lynn Cain who, while gaining 977 yards, had the greatest season ever by a USC fullback.

The national championship probably was decided in the third game of the year when the Trojans traveled to Birmingham, Alabama to play Bear Bryant's Crimson Tide. For years there had been a hue and cry about which team – and which program – was better, and the two schools signed a two-game agreement for 1977 and 1978. Alabama had come to the Coliseum and lost 21-10 in 1977. It would be different in Dixie, the Tide's rooters boasted - but it wasn't. This time USC won 24-14, as McDonald threw a pair of fourth quarter touchdowns to Williams, after White's 40-yard TD run had given USC a 7-0 lead. He finished with 199 yards on 29 carries. Yet at season's end there still was a huge controversy, because the Associated Press pollsters, writers, and

Charles White, carried 15 times for 120 yards, one a 60-yard TD run.

Bell broke Simpson's one-game record with 51 carries in a 347-yard day in USC's tough 23-14 victory over Washington State. The Trojans had a 14-0 lead, saw the game tied 14-14 in the third quarter, and then scored the last nine points, six of them on Bell's nine-yard run as the defense forced the Cougars into three turnovers, and two of them were turned into scores.

White gave USC fans a second glimpse of the future during a 56-0 rout of Oregon State when he replaced Bell, who left the game in the first quarter with an injury, and rushed for 107 yards, caught two passes for 51 yards, and scored four times. Two weeks later the Trojans earned their eighth trip in 11 years to the Rose Bowl with a 24-14 victory over UCLA as Bell ran 36 times for 167 yards, 120 of those in the second half when USC was forced to turn back a series of UCLA rallies.

"We're back where we belong – in Pasadena," Robinson said after the game, but he still hadn't forgotten about his final regular season opponent, Notre Dame, because the Trojans polished off the Irish 17-13 in a fumble-marred game. Bell, in what Robinson called "his finest hour," gained only 75 yards on 21 carries but spent part of the

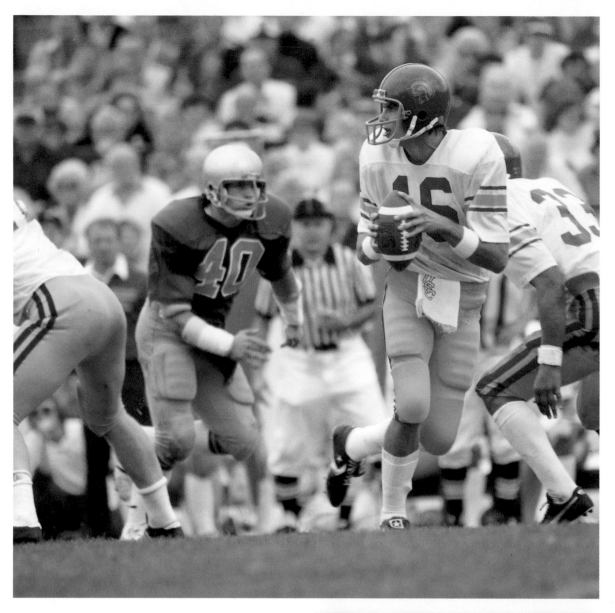

Left: *Quarterback Paul McDonald led USC to a No. 1 ranking in his first season as a starter in 1978, and the Trojans lost only one game in two seasons while he ran the offense. He is the school's No. 4 all-time passer with 4138 yards and 37 TD passes.*

Left: *While tailback Charles White was setting new standards for USC tailbacks in 1978, fullback Lynn Cain (left) not only was a capable blocker in front of him, but also set a rushing record for USC fullbacks with 977 yards.*

broadcasters from across the country selected Alabama as its national champion, despite the fact that the Trojans had really settled matters on the field.

White, like the tailbacks who preceded him at USC, was a yardage machine. He had two games in 1978 of over 200 yards, another of over 190 yards, and five more between 150 and 190. Other than the loss to Arizona State, the Trojans were pushed only in three games – a 13-7 victory over Stanford during which White had 205 yards, his second best day of the year, and scored what became the winning touchdown; 17-10 over UCLA when McDonald completed seven of the 10 passes he threw, two of them for both USC touchdowns while White added 145 rushing yards; and in the finale against Notre Dame when Frank Jordan's 37-yard field goal with two seconds to play spoiled a three-touchdown comeback by Joe Montana and gave USC a 27-25 victory. Had the Irish disdained two missed passes for two-point conversions in favor of placement kicks, they would have come away with a tie.

The Trojans wrapped up their championship season with a 17-10 victory over Michigan in the Rose Bowl as McDonald threw a nine-yard TD pass to Hoby Brenner for a 7-0 lead; White, who gained 99 yards on 32 carries, got the second for a 14-3 lead; and Jordan added a 35-yard field goal a few minutes later for a 17-3 advantage. As was often the case, Robinson used his passing attack sparingly, and McDonald threw only nine passes and completed four.

White was a unanimous All-America choice on a team that also sported such future NFL stars as linemen Anthony Munoz, Brad Budde, and Pat Howell, another were unanimous choice, the eleventh and twelfth players in USC history to be so honored.

USC and Alabama battled for the national title for the third time in four seasons in 1979, and only a 21-21 tie against Stanford cost the Trojans a second straight title – as well as a perfect season. They led Stanford 21-0 in the first half, and didn't do a thing in the second half as Stanford quarterback Turk Schonert passed for two scores and got the tie-maker on a 10-yard run in the fourth quarter. The Tide went 12-0 and was the top choice of both wire services, with USC finishing second in both polls.

White, who gained 221 of the Trojans' 295 rushing yards against Stanford, had a brilliant senior season in 1979, and became the third USC tailback in 14 years to win the Heisman Trophy. He was the first Southern Cal back ever to break the 2000-yard rushing mark for a single season with 2050 – and he didn't even play in the season's second game against Oregon State after being hurt early in the opener against Texas Tech. (A young sophomore named Marcus Allen stepped in and gained 105 yards in that game.)

After that, there was only one game – a 50-21 victory over Washington State – in which he failed to gain less than 150 yards, and he had 17 for 143 in that one before Robinson cleared his bench early. White caught fire in four games during the middle of the season – 261 in 44 carries (and four touchdowns) in a 42-23 victory over Notre Dame; 243 in 38 tries in USC's 24-17 win against Washington; 198 yards in 44 carries in a 24-14 win over California; and the Stanford game. In the final regular season game, he nailed 194 yards in 35 tries as USC crushed UCLA 49-14.

White saved one more great effort for the final game of his career – 247 yards in 39 carries and the winning touchdown in USC's 17-16 victory over Ohio State in the Rose Bowl.

It wasn't all White that season, though, because McDonald was equally brilliant in his own right. Most importantly, in two sea-

Opposite: *USC trailed 16-10 with five minutes to play in the 1980 Rose Bowl against Ohio State when Charles White took over and gained 71 yards in an 83-yard drive, and scored the winning touchdown in a 17-16 victory.*

Above left: *The USC Marching Band has played for 10 presidents and appeared in five movies. Its alumni include Herb Alpert, Henry Mancini, Quincy Jones, Diana Ross, and Neil Diamond.*

Above: *USC's cheerleaders have always epitomized everything blonde and beautiful in southern California.*

sons he led the Trojans to a 21-1-1 record and set 17 NCAA, Pac-10, and USC passing records. In 1979 he threw a touchdown pass in every game but the tie against Stanford – 18 in all – and wound up with the highest completion percentage in USC history (62.1). His 2223 yards on 164 completions in 264 attempts were the most ever by any USC passer.

The White-McDonald combination usually called the day for Southern Cal, such as in the Trojans' 17-12 victory over LSU at Baton Rouge when McDonald passed eight yards to Williams for the winning touchdown with just 32 seconds to play. USC had trailed 12-3 going into the final quarter, but White scored on a four-yard run before McDonald's game-winner. The Trojans were tied 14-14 against California in the fourth quarter before McDonald set up Eric Hipp's go-ahead 45-yard field goal, and White nailed down the win with a five-yard TD run. McDonald also threw a pair of TD passes against Washington that helped the Trojans to a 17-17 tie in the last quarter before Marcus Allen ran 10 yards for the winning score.

Allen's star was on the rise even as White outshone every running back in the country in 1979, and two years later, in the most brilliant single season performance by any running back in USC history, Allen became the fourth Heisman Trophy winner for USC. He gained a school record 2427 yards in 1981, with a crushing 433 carries – more than some running backs accumulate during an entire college career – and an NCAA-record 213 yards per game average. All of this came from a back who many pro

Below: *In 1981, Marcus Allen was the fourth USC tailback in 16 years to win the Heisman Trophy. No other school has more winners of college football's most prestigious individual trophy. The Oakland Raiders scoffed at reports that Allen was "too slow," and made him their No. 1 draft pick in 1981.*

Left: *Allen gained a record 2427 yards from rushing during his senior season in 1981. He finished as the Trojans' No. 2 all-time rusher with 4810 yards after just two of his four varsity seasons as a starter, and set an NCAA record with eleven 200-yard rushing games.*

scouts said was not fast enough for the NFL, a doubt he later dispelled with a fine career with the Oakland/Los Angeles Raiders.

His figures were almost superhuman as the Trojans won 9 of 12 games. He gained more than 200 yards in his first five games, and in seven overall, with 289 in 44 carries against Washington State his best, closely followed by 274 in 40 carries against Indiana. In the season's first big shootout, against Oklahoma and its high-powered wishbone offense, Allen picked up 208 yards in a 28-24 Trojan victory and scored two touchdowns as USC, helped by five lost Oklahoma fumbles (the Sooners fumbled 10 times during the game) came from a 24-14 deficit in the fourth quarter for the win. Allen had a three-yard TD run, and John Mazur passed seven yards to Fred Cornwell with two seconds to play for the game-winning TD.

USC hit a dead spot against Arizona after Allen's 74-yard run helped them to a 10-0 lead after the first quarter. They didn't score again and lost 13-10; and later lost the Pac-10 title, 13-3 against Washington.

But those disappointing moments were rare. Against Notre Dame, Allen broke a scoreless tie with a 14-yard TD run in the third quarter, and after the Irish tied it, Todd Spencer ran 26 yards for the winning score with 4:26 left in the last quarter. With the usual "bragging rights" on the line against UCLA, Allen ran 40 times for 219 yards and led a 10-0 fourth quarter comeback by scoring the winning touchdown on a five-yard run in a 22-21 victory. Like their other daredevil wins, the Trojans brought this one right down to the wire as George Achica blocked a Uclan field goal try on the final play of the game to preserve the triumph.

Thus ended the Era of the USC Tailback – two decades during which four players brought more renown to southern California and its style of football than any quartet of backs in the school's history.

6. New Faces of the Eighties and Nineties

Below: *Quarterback Sean Salisbury led the Trojans in passing in 1982-83 and again in 1985 after missing a season with injuries.*

Southern California football went through an exhausting two decades during the sixties and seventies, and it was unreasonable to assume that such a parade of great players as Mike Garrett, O.J. Simpson, Anthony Davis, Ricky Bell, Charles White, and Marcus Allen could continue indefinitely. Yet the Trojans stayed very competitive with a wave of new faces throughout the eighties and into the nineties – with one big difference: Instead of great running backs, the stars of these teams were good passing quarterbacks like Sean Salisbury, Rodney Peete, and Todd Marinovich.

The results weren't too different, either, because the Trojans still were a fixture in the Rose Bowl, and had jaunts to six other post-season games after John Robinson left for the NFL. Three of those post-season jaunts came with Robinson's successor, Ted Tollner, as head coach – a Pac-10 title in 1984 in his second season as head coach that earned the Trojans a Rose Bowl trip, then one to the Aloha Bowl in 1985, and finally, a trip to the Citrus Bowl in 1987.

Tollner stumbled to a 4-6-1 season in 1983, but produced a 9-3 team the following year that won USC's 24th conference championship. It wasn't always easy – in fact, it took a different approach this time with a stingy defense, led by linebacker Duane Bickett, and a bit of good fortune when substitute quarterback Tim Green decided to pass up a redshirt season. That really saved the Trojans from a disaster after Salisbury was injured and lost for the season in the second game against Arizona State. USC held on to win, 6-3, on a pair of Steve Jordan field goals and some clutch quarterbacking by redshirt freshman Kevin McLean.

The following week, McLean's inexperience showed in a 22-3 loss to Louisiana State and Green got the job for the rest of the season. He led the Trojans to six straight victories en route to the Rose Bowl, starting the journey at Pullman, Washington for the first time in 29 years, and came away with a 29-27 victory over Washington State. Just to show that old habits don't die, the running game worked, too, as Fred Crutcher gained 171 yards, the first of his four 100-yard games that season.

Bickett and the defense also stepped forward the following week in a 19-9 win over Oregon, starting a string of four straight victories (and six of the first seven) in which opponents were held to less than 300 yards. Jordan chipped in with four field goals, and then kicked the game-winner a week later in a 17-14 victory over Arizona.

Two weeks later, USC's defense did it again as Neil Hope recorded 18 tackles and

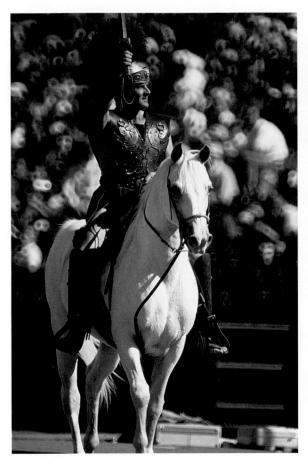

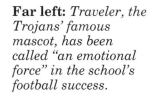

Far left: *Traveler, the Trojans' famous mascot, has been called "an emotional force" in the school's football success.*

Left: *Quarterback Rodney Peete was USC's most exciting quarterback of all time with his running and passing heroics from 1985-88.*

Left: *Coach Ted Tollner led the Trojans to a pair of bowl appearances during his four-year stint as head coach, including a 20-17 victory over Ohio State in the Rose Bowl.*

Bickett had 16, plus a pair of sacks, to pace the Trojans to a 20-11 victory over Stanford. Rarely had any of the USC faithful seen defense as Southern Cal played it that day – protecting a 7-3 third quarter lead, first with a goal line stand, then stopping the Cardinals twice more in USC territory following two turnovers; and finally jump-starting the offense to a 13-point fourth quarter with interceptions that set up a pair of touchdowns.

The run for the Roses ended the following week when the Trojans whipped the top-ranked Washington Huskies 16-7, with a 10-point fourth quarter on Crutcher's touchdown and Jordan's third field goal of the game. The Trojan defense held Washington's 31-points-per-game offense to just 85 rushing yards, and never allowed the Huskies closer than USC's 32-yard line except for a lone TD drive that began on Southern Cal's 38-yard line.

The joy of a Pac-10 title was flattened a bit with season-ending losses against UCLA and Notre Dame, but all was forgiven when the Trojans, in their first trip to the Rose Bowl in five years, defeated Ohio State 20-17. USC's defense limited the Buckeyes' All-America running back Keith Byers to just 59 yards, almost 100 yards below his average, while Green passed for a pair of touchdowns and Jordan kicked a pair of 51-yard field goals, giving him six that year of 50 yards or more.

Though Tollner brought his team to two more post-season games in the following seasons, he found that life at Troy was filled with expectations that were much too high and patience that was much too low – in other words, USC fans were spoiled and didn't appreciate 6-6 (1985) and 7-5 (1987) records. Critics claimed his club was not dominant, that it was too inconsistent and that it didn't produce the super players that fans had gotten used to seeing in the previous two decades. They also grumbled loudly about his inability to beat Notre Dame – USC hadn't defeated the Irish since Robinson's final season in 1982 – and a less-than-consistent record against arch-rival UCLA, though they were mollified a bit in 1985 when Rodney Peete's quarterback

Overleaf: *Wide receiver Eric Affholter was one of Rodney Peete's favorite targets and set a school record with 68 receptions for 952 yards and eight touchdowns in 1988. He is second on USC's all-time list with 123 catches.*

Below: *Larry Smith became USC's head coach in 1987.*

Bottom: *Rodney Peete (center) is flanked by four USC Heisman Trophy winners: Charles White, O. J. Simpson, Mike Garrett, and Marcus Allen. Peete finished his college career as USC's top career passer, with 8225 yards and 54 TDs.*

Opposite: *Todd Marinovich was the first starting freshman quarterback in USC history in 1989.*

sneak with 73 seconds to play pulled out a 17-13 victory.

Neither that nor the trips to the Aloha and Citrus bowls were enough, and Tollner was replaced in 1987 by Larry Smith, who had been head coach at the University of Arizona since 1980. Smith came to USC with great credentials, having coached under Bo Schembechler at Miami University in Ohio, the famed "Cradle of Coaches." He was on Schembechler's staff at Michigan as line coach for four years before serving at the University of Arizona as defensive coordinator under Jim Young, who had worked with him at Michigan. He was head coach at Tulane for four years, taking the team to the Liberty Bowl in 1979, and then returned to Arizona as head coach.

His appointment hasn't disappointed USC fans. He started out by making regular trips to the Rose Bowl – he was the first USC coach, and only the second in history, to take a team to the Rose Bowl in each of his first three seasons. His 1987 team turned in an 8-4 record, but in USC's football centennial season, 1988, he vied with Notre Dame for the national championship. His big weapon was Rodney Peete, a nifty, mobile quarterback who could run as well as he could pass – and he did both in All-America fashion. Smith backed him up with a good running game that produced four different 100-yard rushers in games during that season; wide receiver Eric Affholter; and a solid defense that featured defensive backs Mark Carrier and Cleveland Colter playing behind linemen Tim Ryan and Dan Owens, and linebacker Scott Ross.

But Peete was to this team what the great tailbacks of the sixties and seventies had been to their teams. He passed for 200 or more yards in seven games, twice going over 300 yards, and had three games in which he threw three touchdown passes. Affholter twice caught three touchdown passes, in a rollicking 38-15 victory over Arizona and 41-20 against Oregon State, and had an eight-catch day for 135 yards in a 50-0 win against Arizona State when Peete rolled up a career-high 361 passing yards.

Peete also had a flair for the dramatic, beginning in the season's second game when he threw the winning touchdown pass to John Jackson with 79 seconds to play in a 24-20 victory over Stanford. The following week, he was matched against Oklahoma's Jamelle Holieway and led the fourth-ranked Trojans to a 23-7 victory over the third-ranked Sooners. He passed for 189 yards and ran for 22 yards on a third-and-20 situation that keyed the first touchdown drive. USC's defense shut down Holieway and the Sooners' big wishbone attack, allowing only 89 rushing yards and forcing six turnovers.

The Rose Bowl was on the line when the second-ranked Trojans played sixth-ranked UCLA, and for the second straight year – and the ninth consecutive time when the two met to decide the issue – USC won. Peete was hospitalized with the measles and missed practice the week before the game, but he still completed 16 of 28 passes for 189 yards and a touchdown and scored another in a 31-22 victory. Defensively, Scott Ross had a game-high 14 tackles as USC's defense held an opponent under 100 rushing yards for the sixth straight game.

The following week, a national championship was at stake against Notre Dame and its slick-running quarterback Tony Rice. The media made this as much a Peete versus Rice shootout as one between the nation's two top teams, and in both cases

Rice and Notre Dame carried the day in a 27-10 victory. Though USC dominated the game offensively (356-253 in total yards, 21-8 in first downs, 84-50 in plays), the Trojans suffered four turnovers, two resulting in Notre Dame touchdowns; a separated shoulder hampered Peete, though he completed 23 of 44 passes for 225 yards; and Rice had 86 rushing yards, including a 65-yard TD.

Smith discovered that Schembechler hadn't taught him every lesson at Michigan, as Bo rallied the Wolverines from a 14-3 halftime deficit and upended the Trojans 22-14 in the Rose Bowl. Peete scored both USC touchdowns, but this was offset by five turnovers and a penalty-marred performance that contributed to USC's season-low 298 yards in offense.

The 1989 season introduced Todd Marinovich, whose father Marv had been captain of USC's 1962 national champions, as the next of the Trojans' bright new quarterbacks. He was one of the most heralded quarterback recruits in college football history, with a yard-long list of honors during his career at Capistrano Valley High School in Mission Viejo, California. Few quarterbacks in the game's history have been as well trained and conditioned as he. His father operated an athletic research center, and had literally raised his son to play at USC. He had dozens of experts work on all aspects of his son's physical conditioning in such specific areas as speed, agility, strength, flexibility, quickness, body control, endurance, nutrition, vision, throwing, and psychology.

In 1989, Marinovich became the first freshman quarterback to start a season opener at USC since World War II, and both he and the Trojans were stunned when Illinois rallied from a 13-0 deficit midway through the last quarter and upset USC 14-13. Smith realized immediately that his young quarterback simply could not carry the entire load by himself, so he fell back on what all past USC teams had done best – he ran the ball.

The results were dramatic. Marinovich gained only 92 yards in USC's 56-10 victory over Utah State, but the Trojans unveiled a new running sensation in Ricky Ervins, a 5' 8", 180-pound tailback who rolled for 180 yards, the first of nine 100-yard games in 1989. Smith backed him with 6' 0", 225-pound fullback Leroy Holt, and it was like old times again – except that Marinovich added a brand new dimension and produced passing yardage never before achieved by any USC quarterback.

Obviously more relaxed and comfortable knowing that he had other offensive weapons, he rolled off seven straight 200-yard passing games, including back-to-back 300-yard performances against Notre Dame and Stanford. He exploded for a four-touchdown performance in a 42-3 win over Ohio State, and later in the year had three in a victory over Oregon State and a loss against Notre Dame. He kept an entire nation on edge against the Irish in an emotion-packed game at South Bend, and had his team ahead 17-7 at the half en route to setting a school record for most completions (33), including 14 for 142 of his 333 yards to flanker John Jackson. But the Irish rallied to win 28-24 as the Trojans' top-ranked rushing defense fell apart, though Marinovich brought his team to within seven yards of a winning touchdown in the final minute of the game before missing on three pass plays.

Marinovich's yardage output cooled off in the final three games of the year, including 154 yards in a 10-10 tie against UCLA. But he produced 178 yards in the Rose Bowl and

Below: *In 1989, 5'8" junior tailback Ricky Ervins belied his size with nine 100-yard games, including 180 against Utah State and 173 against UCLA, leading the Trojans with 1269 yards for the season. "I'm like a pinball, bouncing off everyone," he said.*

Ervins, the game's MVP, rushed for 173 en route to a 17-10 victory over Michigan, spoiling Schembechler's final game as the Wolverines' head coach. After a penalty had nullified a daring fourth-down fake punt run to USC's 30-yard line by Michigan with six minutes to play, the Trojans moved 75 yards for their clinching score. Marinovich added a 20-yard, third-down pass to keep the drive alive, and Ervins ran 10 yards for the winning touchdown with just 70 seconds to play.

Marinovich had a tough time of it in 1990, many believing that he was suffering from too much hands-on programming from his father. During the middle of the season, Smith started Shane Foley at quarterback for the first time and he led USC to a 13-6 victory over Arizona State. He later passed for two touchdowns and ran for a third in a 56-7 win over Oregon State, and finished up in the Trojans' 17-16 loss to Michigan State in the John Hancock Bowl.

Marinovich and the Trojans started out well, winning key early games against Penn State and Ohio State. He threw two TD passes in the 19-14 victory against the Nittany Lions in the first regular season game ever between the two schools. In a 35-26 win at Ohio State, tailback Ricky Ervins scored twice and had 199 yards rushing. Marinovich was at his best in one of the most thrilling games ever played in the UCLA series, passing 23 yards to Johnnie Morton, who made a diving catch for the winning touchdown in the final 16 seconds of a 45-42 victory. The 87 points were the most ever scored in this series, and almost half of them came in the wild fourth quarter when Marinovich's 21-yard TD pass to Morton gave USC a 38-35 lead with 3:09 to play. But the Bruins went ahead 42-38 with 1:19 to play before Marinovich directed a five-play, 75-yard TD drive that featured completions of 27 and 22 yards to Gary Wellman that set up the winning score.

Above: *Leroy Holt was a hard-working fullback in 1989 whose blocking led the way for Ricky Ervins. He also gained more than 500 yards, including 160 against California, and was the team's most inspirational player with his emotional pre-game pep talks.*

7. The Fighting Irish and Battlin' Bruins

Below: *When the Trojans returned home from South Bend after defeating Notre Dame 16-14 in 1931, thousands turned out for a huge ticker tape parade down Spring Street in Los Angeles.*

Rivalries are the spice of college football, and when two teams vie for one area's loyalties, then it becomes a pitched battle for bragging rights that will last for 365 days – happy ones for the winners, excruciating ones for the losers. That is how Southern California regards its Westwood neighbor, UCLA, as the two battle for the love of L.A. each season.

But while taking care of the home front is one order of business for the Trojans, they also have an annual date with their fiercest non-conference rival, Notre Dame, a rivalry that has been flourishing since 1926 when Knute Rockne was in the midst of his great tenure at South Bend.

As you might expect with anything having to do with Rockne, there are a couple of colorful stories about how the rivalry began. One, it is said, was the result of a promise that Rockne had exacted from Howard Jones to play one of his teams in a rematch after Jones's Iowa team had beaten Notre Dame 10-7 in 1921. In the meantime, Jones became head coach at USC in 1925, partly on the recommendation of Rockne who had turned down Southern Cal officials because he was already

under contract with Notre Dame. Rockne had juiced up Southern Cal by an offhand remark following his team's victory over Stanford in the 1925 Rose Bowl, while noting that USC's Elmer Henderson simply could not beat arch-rival California. "I'll have to come out here and show USC how to beat a team from the North," Rockne cracked.

Southern Cal thought he was serious and was mightily chagrined when he turned them down. But Jones was so grateful for Rockne's recommendation, it is said, that he fulfilled Rockne's desire to have his team play on the West Coast and scheduled a game in the Coliseum in 1926.

In another version of the story, it was Southern California which wanted the Irish to come to Los Angeles. Graduate manager of athletics Gwynn Wilson, with his new bride Marion, went to Lincoln, Nebraska where Notre Dame was playing the University of Nebraska in the final game of the 1925 season, to try and sell Rockne on the idea. His timing couldn't have been worse, because Notre Dame lost the game 17-0 and Rockne said his school was already unhappy with the team's extensive traveling schedule. But he invited Wilson and his wife to travel back to

Left: *Tommy Trojan stands at the center of the USC campus. The bronze statue was presented in 1930 at the University's 50th Jubilee.*

Left: *Electronic football, early-1930s style was set up so that those not attending Notre Dame-USC in South Bend could still follow the action. The ball's position on the field was moved along the gridiron and lights by individual players denoted who made the play.*

Overleaf: *O. J. Simpson (32) was always at his best in big rivalry games such as USC's 24-7 victory over Notre Dame in 1967.*

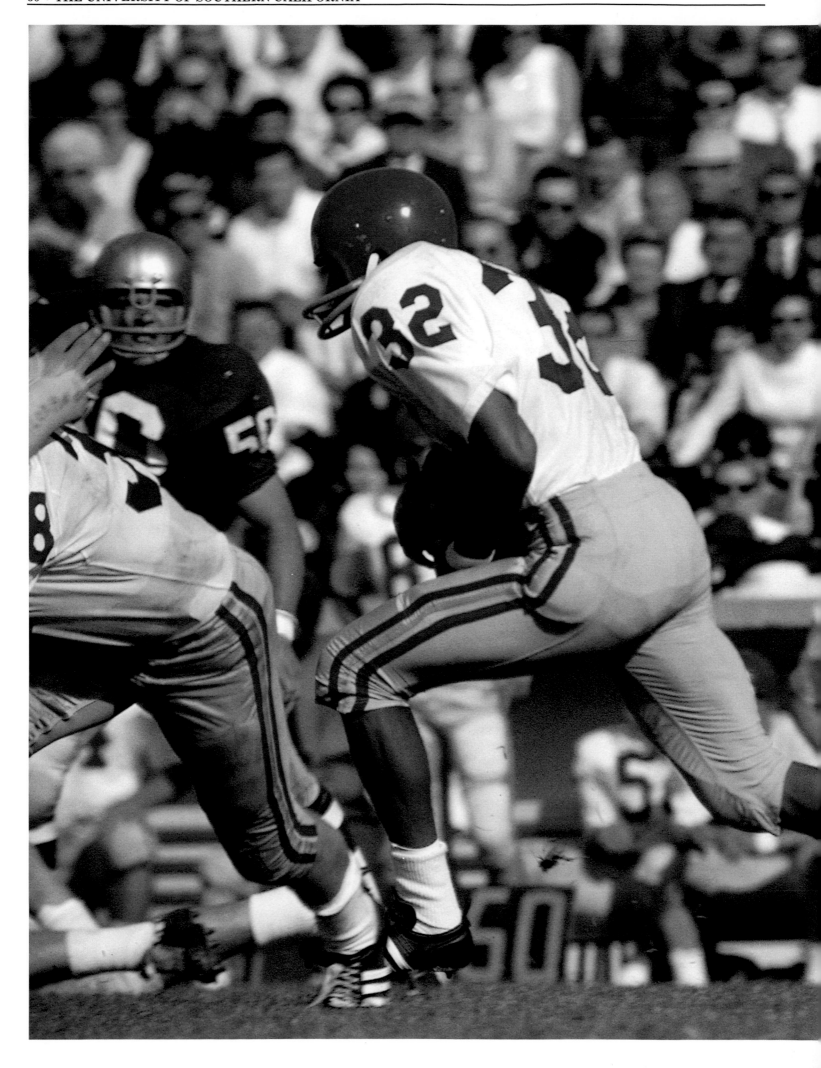

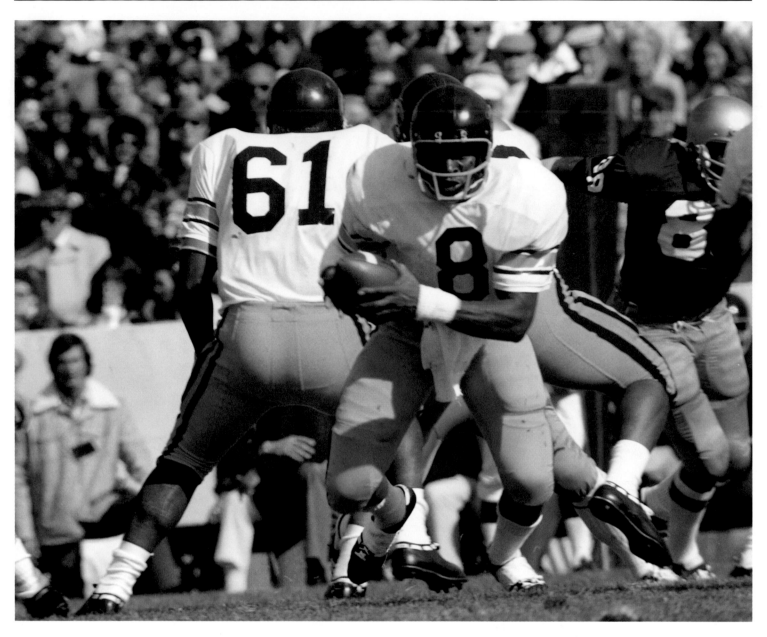

Above: *Quarterback Vince Evans rolls out in the 1975 edition of USC's greatest non-conference rivalry.*

Chicago on the train with his team, where Mrs. Wilson and Mrs. Rockne struck up a fast friendship. Marion Wilson described in rapturous detail how wonderful it would be if Notre Dame could come to the West Coast, and rhapsodized about such trimmings as baskets of fresh fruits and flowers in the hotel rooms, sunny, warm days and nights, and a brand new world for the players. Bonnie Rockne liked the idea and so convinced her husband, it is said, that two weeks later Nebraska was dropped from Notre Dame's 1926 schedule and replaced by USC.

Whichever version is correct is immaterial now, because the rivalry has been significant for both schools. In 1926, USC blew a 12-7 fourth-quarter lead when a substitute named Art Parisien, the last back on the Irish roster, came into the game and began throwing left-handed passes that moved Notre Dame to the winning touchdown on a 20-yard pass to Johnny Niemiec in the final seconds. The following year, more than 100,000 persons crammed

Chicago's Soldier Field and watched some more Irish "luck," as Notre Dame won 7-6 because the Trojans failed to kick an extra point after Morley Drury passed to Russ Saunders for a touchdown.

Southern Cal got its first victory in 1928, taking a 20-0 lead when Tony Steponovich turned the tables on Niemiec and returned one of his passes 18 yards for a TD; Don Williams threw a touchdown pass to Marger Aspit; and Saunders whipped across on a beautifully executed "run to daylight" play. Southern Cal won the game 27-14, and with the victory came a burst of national recognition far greater than the school had earned with its other successes.

The last game Rockne ever coached at Notre Dame was against USC in Los Angeles in 1930 and had a typical Rockne-esque plot. Rockne wanted Jones to believe that Dan Hanley, who was slow and inexperienced, would play fullback when in fact he had decided to move Bucky O'Connor, a speedy reserve halfback, to the position.

Rockne knew that some Los Angeles

writers watched his team work out in Tucson, so he ordered O'Connor and Hanley to exchange jerseys. He even had O'Connor flub a couple of plays during the drill so he could moan about "Hanley's" inability to do the job. But when photographers wanted pictures, he ordered the two inside to exchange jerseys again, then ran a couple of plays, and called off practice.

The scam almost came apart after the Irish finished their day-before drill at the Coliseum when Bill Henry, the *Times* football writer, asked to interview Hanley. There was no time to make a switch again, so Rockne introduced O'Connor as Dan Hanley – the inflection of his voice such that O'Connor knew who he was to be – and they pulled it off again. The real success came the next day when O'Connor played

himself, scored three touchdowns, and the Irish handed USC only its second loss that year, 27-0. Nearly five months later, Rockne was killed in an airplane crash while en route to Los Angeles on a business trip.

When Jones later found out about the switch, it didn't change his feelings about Rockne one bit. The following year in South Bend, Gus Shaver led a furious last-ditch drive that ended with Johnny Baker kicking a 33-yard field goal with 63 seconds to play for a 16-14 Trojan victory. Unbridled joy swept USC's dressing room after the game and for the entire long train ride back to Los Angeles, where a huge celebration followed.

But there also had been a somber moment, because Jones had loaded his players onto a bus after the game and had

Left: *Quarterback Paul McDonald completed 21 of 32 passes for 311 yards and a pair of TDs in the Trojans' 42-23 victory over Notre Dame in 1979.*

gone directly to the cemetery where Rockne had been interred just a few months before. While the joys of this incredible victory – USC had overcome a 14-0 deficit – still filled their minds, they also reverently followed their coach in a quiet graveside ceremony to honor his friend and rival.

The series has never been dull and often the unexpected is all anyone can expect, as happened in 1948 when Notre Dame, which hadn't lost a game since 1945, came to Los Angeles as a three-touchdown favorite against Jeff Cravath's 6-3 Trojans. Notre Dame obviously didn't respect the Trojans and fumbled and bumbled around for most of the game, leading only 7-0 going into the fourth quarter. Given this life, USC rose up and grabbed a 14-7 lead on a pair of touchdowns by Bill Martin.

Notre Dame halfback Bill Gay, oblivious to the disaster that stared his team in the face, asked an official how much time was left after Martin's second TD. When told there were two minutes and 35 seconds, he replied: "That's more than enough time if they will just kick it to me." USC did, and Gay returned the kickoff 86 yards to the Trojan 13-yard line. A pass interference penalty gave the Irish a first down on the two-yard line and two plays later, Red Sitko scored and Steve Oracko kicked the tie-making extra point. Notre Dame had escaped with a 14-14 tie, an unbeaten streak of 28 games still intact, but Southern Cal won the bigger battle because that

tie cost the Irish a third straight national championship.

Of course, dramatic finishes are part of every rivalry, and there have been plenty in this series. In 1978, Frank Jordan's 37-yard field goal with two seconds to play gave USC a 27-25 victory and spoiled a near-miracle comeback performance by ND's Joe Montana; Todd Spencer's 26-yard touchdown run with 4:52 to play gave USC a 14-7 victory three years later; and Michael Harper, with the ball coming loose as he dove over the goal line with 48 seconds to play, got the winning touchdown in a 17-13 victory in 1982, John Robinson's last game as head coach.

But no game has ever equaled what is still known at USC as "The Comeback." In 1974, USC trailed 24-0 late in the first half, and since the Irish had the nation's top-rated defense, there seemed to be no chance of overcoming such a large deficit. But with 10 seconds to play in the second quarter, Pat Haden passed to Anthony Davis for a touchdown, and the Trojans trailed 24-7.

Still, that didn't seem like much until Davis returned the second half kickoff 102 yards for a touchdown. This just opened the flood gates, because Davis scored twice more in the third quarter as part of a 35-point explosion, the other TDs coming on 18- and 45-yard passes from Haden to Johnny McKay. Two minutes after the fourth quarter began, Haden threw his fourth TD pass of the day to Sheldon Diggs,

Right: *Anthony Davis opened USC's stunning second half comeback against Notre Dame in 1974 with a 100-yard kickoff return. The Trojans trailed 24-6, and this was the first of five third quarter TDs that led to an eventual 55-24 victory. Davis scored four touchdowns, the most by any player in this series.*

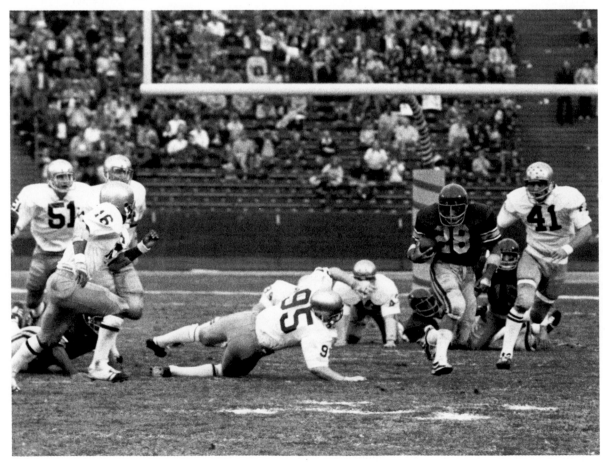

and Charles Phillips returned an interception 58 yards for a TD – 55 points in just 17 and a half minutes, and the Trojans romped home 55-24 winners.

Nothing of that magnitude ever happened to the Trojans in their crosstown series against UCLA, but that does not mean that there haven't been some wild times since the two teams have faced each other continuously since 1936. USC had opened the rivalry in 1929 and 1930 with lopsided 76-0 and 52-0 victories. UCLA was just 10 years old when those first two games were played but by 1936, the Bruins had established themselves in the Pacific Coast Conference, and were considered very capable of beating USC. The two teams resumed their series on Thanksgiving Day, and 85,000 people came to the Coliseum to watch the favored Trojans fight for their lives. They trailed 7-0 before sophomore Ambrose Schindler led a third quarter charge that ended with Jimmy Jones's tie-making touchdown and a 7-7 standoff. But the rivalry was firmly established, and from that day to the present, the teams have delighted Los Angeles with this rivalry, first when the teams played annually in the Coliseum, and since the mid-1980s when UCLA plays host in its home in the Rose Bowl. During World War II (1943-45), the teams played each other twice each season to minimize travel and maintain a full schedule.

The coveted prize of this rivalry, in addition to a year's bragging rights, has been the Victory Bell since 1942. It was originally taken from a retired Southern

Right: *The rivalry with UCLA always has been tightly fought. Twenty-six of the 60 games have been decided by a touchdown or less. In 1981 and 1982, the teams traded one-point victories.*

Above: *USC's Homer Beatty recovers a UCLA fumble behind his own goal line in the 1936 Thanksgiving Day match, which was played to a 7-7 tie. The two teams would meet annually thereafter, forming a hotly-contested rivalry which has produced some of the most exciting games ever played in southern California.*

Pacific freight locomotive and given to UCLA in 1939 by its alumni association to toll after every Uclan victory. In 1942, a group of USC students masquerading as UCLA fans offered to help load the bell onto a truck for its return to the Westwood campus. Their offer was accepted, and when the job was completed, the UCLA students suddenly saw the truck and its prize heading away. UCLA searched in vain and finally agreed to a meeting with USC to discuss terms of return. USC made it simple: The Trojans would return the bell if UCLA agreed to designate it as the winning trophy for the USC-UCLA game. UCLA could only agree, and the bell has been passed back and forth between the two campuses ever since.

Often, the winner of that game also played for a Rose Bowl berth such as in 1939 when both teams, with perfect records, played to the most famous scoreless tie in the series history, before more than 103,000 persons – the largest crowd ever to see a game west of the Mississippi to that time. UCLA, led by All-America running back

Kenny Washington and future major league baseball star Jackie Robinson, disdained a potential game-winning field goal from USC's five-yard line in the final 10 seconds of the game in favor of a touchdown. In the huddle, five players wanted to try the kick and five wanted to try for a TD, so QB Kenny Matthews cast the deciding vote for a TD. But Trojan Bob Robertson knocked down Washington's pass intended for Bob MacPherson to preserve the tie and Southern Cal went on to play – and beat – Tennessee in the Rose Bowl.

Thirteen years later, in 1952, the teams lined up to decide another Rose Bowl berth. Both teams were unbeaten, but USC was given a slight edge on the basis of its great defense. The game also was a duel of the West Coast's two pre-eminent backs, Jim Sears of USC and Paul Cameron, the tailback on Red Sanders's flashy single wing attack. Sears's fumble on a rainy day led to a 3-0 lead by UCLA in the first quarter. A short time later, the Trojans' Al Carmichael broke around end to UCLA's 36-yard line with a 34-yard run, and when he was

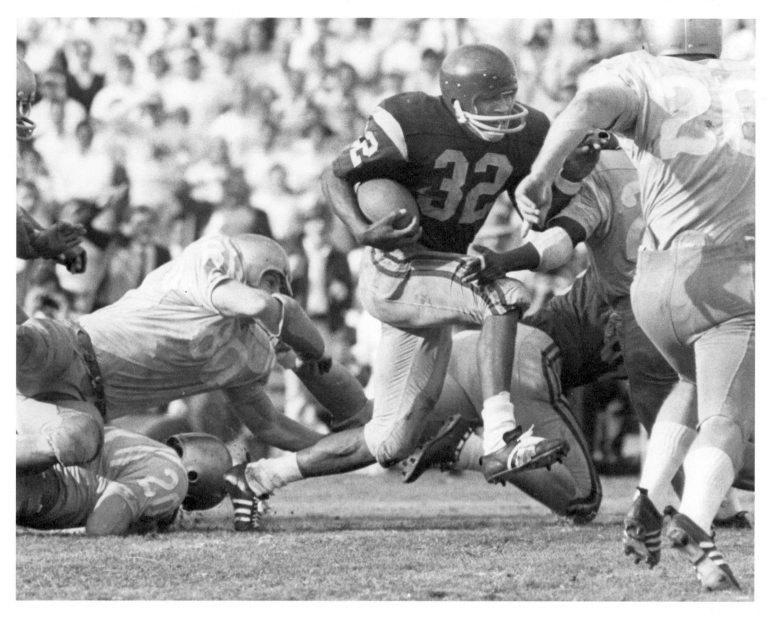

hemmed in, lateraled the ball to Sears who completed the 70-yard play for a 7-3 lead. But UCLA went ahead in a nine-point second quarter on a safety and Billy Stits's TD run before USC put the game away in the third quarter. At the time, UCLA was on a drive deep into Trojan territory before Elmer Willhoite intercepted Cameron's pass and raced 72 yards to UCLA's eight-yard line. On a fourth down play from the four, Sears passed to Carmichael for the winning score. Although USC had its perfect season spoiled the following week by Notre Dame, the Trojans went to the Rose Bowl and defeated Wisconsin 7-0 for the first win by a West Coast team over the Big Ten.

If it wasn't a Rose Bowl berth at stake, then sometimes a clock meant the difference for the two teams, such as in 1958 when USC salvaged a mediocre season by overcoming a UCLA lead when Luther Hayes returned a kickoff 74 yards for one TD and Tom Mauldin ran for the two-point conversion late in the fourth quarter to get USC a 15-15 tie. The game featured a great

duel between UCLA tailback Bill Kilmer and USC's Don Buford. Kilmer later was a star quarterback for the Washington Redskins and Buford had a distinguished career in major league baseball.

The clock was an important player in 1969 when the Trojans' Jimmy Jones hit Sam Dickerson with a 32-yard TD pass in the corner of the end zone with just 1:32 to play, giving the Trojans a 14-12 victory and a berth in the Rose Bowl. In 1977, Frank Jordan kicked a 38-yard field goal with two seconds to play, giving USC a 29-27 victory and knocking UCLA out of the Rose Bowl.

In the 1980s, Rodney Peete worked some of his magical finishes against UCLA. In 1985, he scored the winning touchdown on a one-yard sneak with 73 seconds to play as USC won 17-13. Two years later, he passed 33 yards to Eric Affholter, who made a juggling catch in the end zone with 7:59 to play to cap a 17-point fourth quarter in a 17-13 victory, nailing down another Rose Bowl berth for the Trojans.

But of all the games and all the plays in this storied series, one stands out – O.J.

Above: *O. J. Simpson (32) sprints 13 yards to score USC's second touchdown in the 1967 game versus UCLA. Simpson's 64-yard run in the fourth quarter brought the Trojans a 21-20 victory in one of the most memorable games in this classic rivalry.*

Above: *Anthony Davis ends a 10-yard run for the first touchdown in USC's 23-13 victory over UCLA in 1973 that sent the Trojans to the Rose Bowl. No. 22 is USC receiver Lynn Swann.*

Right: *USC football was the first team to involve its fans in the color and pageantry during the game with their famous flashing card displays that showed everything from the school's name to pictures of mountains and oceans.*

Simpson's 64-yard touchdown run with 10:38 to play in the fourth quarter of the 1967 game that gave the Trojans a 21-20 victory, a Rose Bowl berth, and a national championship. Still considered one of the most famous runs in college football history, the play climaxed a great duel between The Juice and UCLA quarterback Gary Beban, who won the Heisman Trophy that season.

Beban's 20-yard TD pass to Dave Nuttall broke a 14-14 tie in the fourth quarter, but Zenon Andrusyshyn missed the extra point. On their next possession, USC faced a third down at the 34-yard line when quarterback Toby Page, noting the UCLA defense shifting into double coverage on the wide receivers, switched a pass play to USC's bread-and-butter "23 Blast," which sent Simpson through the middle.

The call was perfect. Tackle Mike Taylor and guard Steve Lehner blasted open a hole and Simpson, with his world class speed, whooshed through, picked up downfield blocks from Danny Scott, Earl McCullough, and Ron Drake and ran untouched into the end zone. Rikki Aldridge kicked the deciding extra point.

8. Happy New Year, Pasadena

Below: *The Trojans completed a 10-1 season in 1931 by defeating Tulane in the 1932 Rose Bowl 21-12 as Ernie Pinckert (right, above), one of the greatest backs in USC history, scored twice and John Baker (lower, right) kicked three extra points.*

On most days, it is about an hour's drive from the University of Southern California campus to the Rose Bowl in Pasadena. But for each of 27 years since 1923, it has taken the Trojans about three months to make the trip – and they have made it more often than any other Pac-10 team.

Called "the granddaddy of all bowls," the Rose Bowl was first played in 1902 when Michigan coach Fielding Yost brought his point-a-minute team to California and defeated Stanford 49-0. That shock didn't subside until 1916 when the Tournament of Roses committee decided to jazz up its New Year's Day celebration and started the annual series. In 1923, a new Rose Bowl Stadium had just been completed and the University of California was invited to represent the West Coast. But the Golden Bears declined and USC, which had won nine of 10 games under coach Elmer Henderson, got the bid and defeated Penn State 14-3.

This game wasn't without unusual incidents. First, Penn State got caught up in the traffic which still jams the narrow roads in and out of the Arroyo Seco, and was 45 minutes late for the game. USC's first touchdown was set up by Harold Galloway, who caught a pass while laying flat on his back at the two-yard line. And with the later start, the game was concluded by the light of the moon, and it is said that writers had to finish their stories by matchlight.

University of Pittsburgh coach Jock Sutherland brought his teams to the Rose Bowl in 1930 and 1933, and Howard Jones countered with two of his best and won both

JERRY DALRYMPLE   ORVILLE MOHLER   DONALD ZIMMERMAN   NOLLIE FELTS   ERNIE PINC...   JOHN BAKER

TULANE vs. So. CALIFORNIA

Left: *Marshall Duffield (left) and Russ Saunders combined to pass for 279 yards and four TDs in USC's 47-14 victory over Pitt in the 1930 Rose Bowl. Duffield also scored a pair of touchdowns and kicked an extra point.*

games in convincing fashion. In 1930, quarterbacks Russ Saunders and Marshall Duffield combined to pass for 279 yards and four touchdowns as Jones's first Rose Bowl team won, 47-14. The Panthers, which had been picked to win by Knute Rockne and John Heisman, had geared their defense to stop USC's great running game. So Jones told Saunders to open up his passing game and he produced two touchdowns in the first 10 minutes on a 55-yard pass to Harry Edelson, one of two he caught in the game, and a 25-yard strike to Ernie Pinckert.

That game might well have been won on Pitt's first offensive play. The Panthers' fastest back, Toby Uansa, broke into the clear

and seemed assured of a touchdown, only to be caught from behind at USC's 14-yard line by Saunders, who had been knocked down on the play by Pitt's blockers. He had gotten up and chased down Uansa, stunning the Pitt players who rightly wondered that if USC could catch their best runner from behind, what other chance did they have to win? The Trojans halted that Pitt surge as Pinckert knocked down a fourth-down pass and the Trojan offense took over.

In 1933, quarterback Cotton Warburton scored two touchdowns and the Trojans scored 28 points in the second half by wearing down a lighter Pitt team for a 35-0 victory. Sutherland never forgot those defeats

Above: *Al Krueger catches the most famous touchdown pass in USC's Rose Bowl history, grabbing Doyle Nave's 19-yard throw in the final two minutes behind Duke's Eric Tipton for a 7-3 victory over the previously unbeaten and unscored-upon Blue Devils in the 1939 game.*

and when he brought his team back to the Rose Bowl four years later to play Washington, he had his team driven by bus to a point overlooking the stadium and told his players, "There it is boys, the place where two Pitt teams were beaten by a total of 68 points."

The previous year, 1932, Ernie Pinckert had punctuated the final outing for the Trojans' famed "Thundering Herd" and led them to a 21-12 victory against Bernie Bierman's overmatched Tulane Green Wave. Pinckert ran for touchdowns of 23 and 30 yards to provide enough of a cushion to hold off a late Tulane rally.

The two most memorable Rose Bowl matchups were Southern Cal's back-to-back games against Duke and Tennessee in 1939 and 1940. Neither opponent had allowed a point in compiling perfect

records, an incredible feat regardless of the era. Both teams, coached by Wallace Wade and Gen. Robert Neyland, respectively, held to the same theory of strong defense and an absolute trust in their kicking game to set up scoring opportunities. Duke, which had a great kicker in Eric Tipton, often punted on first down if the ball was inside its 30-yard line, and preferred to back up an opponent gradually until it had fine field position for its offense. Neyland was renowned for his defense and the simplicity of his offense, which was geared not to make any mistakes and to give the defense every opportunity to succeed.

In the 1939 game, Duke still was unscored-upon and led 3-0 with about two minutes to play. Jones had gone with Grenville Lansdell, Mickey Anderson, and Ollie Day as his primary backs for most of the game, but hadn't used Doyle Nave, who was his best passer who had played only occasionally all season.

USC had the ball at the Blue Devils' 39-yard line when Jones, knowing his team would have to pass if it wanted to win, finally sent Nave into the game. Nave told Jones he wanted to utilize the "27 series," which featured end Al Krueger, and he immediately completed his first two throws for a first down. His third play was a completion behind the line to Krueger, who was tackled for a two-yard loss.

About 50 seconds were left when Nave launched the most famous pass in USC bowl history – a 19-yard touchdown to Krueger to the left corner of the end zone. Krueger had slipped Tipton's coverage and Nave let the ball fly even before he reached the end zone, lofting a perfect pass that was caught for a 7-3 victory.

In 1940, the Vols made the first of two forays against USC in the Rose Bowl, coming to the 1940 game with a 23-game winning streak in addition to not having been scored upon in 15 straight games. But the bigger and stronger Trojans, led by reserve

Ambrose Schindler who scored once and passed to Krueger for the other TD, handled them with apparent ease and won 14-0. The victory gave Jones a 5-0 Rose Bowl record. Tennessee returned again in 1945, and got shut out again, 25-0, as Jim Hardy passed for two touchdowns and ran for a third.

After losing to Alabama 34-14 in 1946, all of USC's Rose Bowl adventures have been against Big Ten teams – primarily Ohio State and Michigan, which have represented the Big Ten more often than any of its other teams in the Rose Bowl.

The first game against Michigan was a 49-0 disaster in 1948, but the next time the two met, in 1970, the Trojans, making a record fourth straight Rose Bowl appearance, came away with a 10-3 victory that was marred when Wolverine coach Bo Schembechler suffered a heart attack and had to miss the game. Jimmy Jones's TD pass to Bob Chandler was the victory margin as the Trojans' "Wild Bunch" defense held Michigan to just one field goal.

USC rolled off two consecutive victories over Michigan in 1977 and 1979, with

Below: *Ambrose Schindler scores the first of USC's two touchdowns against Tennessee, another unbeaten and unscored-upon team, in the 1940 Rose Bowl. He passed to Al Krueger, hero of the 1939 victory over Duke, for the second score as the Trojans won 14-0.*

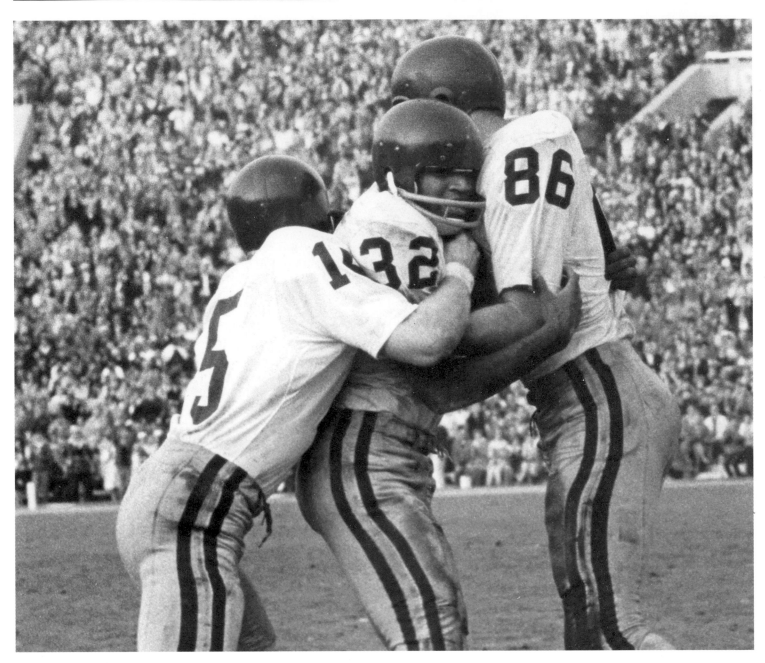

Above: *Toby Page (left) and Bob Miller (right) hug teammate O. J. Simpson after he plunged for USC's second touchdown in the third quarter of the 14-3 victory over Indiana in the 1968 Rose Bowl.*

Opposite: *Sheldon Diggs catches the game-winning two-point conversion pass from quarterback Pat Haden to give USC an 18-17 victory over Ohio State in the 1975 Rose Bowl.*

Charles White having a key role in each. In 1977, he replaced Ricky Bell early in the game and finished with 122 yards and a seven-yard touchdown in a 14-6 come-from-behind win, as John Robinson became only the second coach ever to win a Rose Bowl in his first try. Two years later, White had 99 yards and scored the decisive TD on a disputed call. Replays showed that he hadn't put the ball over the goal line when an official called the touchdown, but it counted anyway in a 17-10 victory.

Disputes seemed commonplace whenever the two teams played. In 1990, Schembechler's final game as Michigan head coach, a controversial penalty nullified a fake punt that gave Michigan a first down at USC's 30-yard line with less than six minutes to play. The Wolverines were forced to punt and the Trojans drove 75 yards in 11 plays, with Ricky Ervins running 14 yards for the winning score with 70 seconds left in a 17-10 victory.

The story was much the same against Ohio State. USC lost its first two Rose Bowl games against the Buckeyes, in 1955 and 1969, and the teams swapped a pair of blowouts in 1973 and 1974. The Trojans defeated Woody Hayes's team 42-17 in 1973 to cap its national championship season, and earned fullback Sam Cunningham the lifelong nickname of "Sam-Bam," as he flew into the end zone for a record-setting four touchdowns. Anthony Davis also ran for 157 yards, and QB Mike Rae passed for 229 yards. In 1974, fullback Pete Johnson scored three times and Heisman Trophy winner Archie Griffin ran for 149 yards as the Bucks overwhelmed USC, 42-21.

When the teams met for a third straight season in 1975, USC came away with another national championship and John McKay won a record-tying fifth Rose Bowl in an 18-17 cliffhanger, fashioned when Pat Haden passed 38 yards to John McKay Jr., the coach's son, for a TD, and hit the win-

Above: *Kevin Williams's 53-yard TD catch gives USC a 7-3 lead against Ohio State in the 1980 Rose Bowl. The final score: USC 17, Ohio State 16.*

quickly threw a pair of TD passes. After an end zone interception by Willie Brown, the Trojans muffed a punting try for a safety, and USC's lead was trimmed to 42-30. With two minutes to play, and the game being played in almost complete darkness, VanderKelen threw his fourth TD pass of the quarter to Pat Richter. USC finally held on to run out the clock.

ning two-point conversion on a pass to Sheldon Diggs.

It took another bit of last-minute heroics from Charles White in 1980 to come up with a 17-16 win for the Trojans over Ohio State. USC jumped off to a 10-0 lead but Ohio State led 16-10 late in the fourth quarter when White, who won the Heisman Trophy that year, took over with 5:21 to play. In six carries, he gained 71 of USC's 83 yards, including a game-winning one-yard touchdown run with 1:32 remaining in the game. His 247 yards in the game set a new bowl record.

There were a couple of other times when the nation's two top-ranked teams played in the Rose Bowl. In 1963, Southern Cal had already been declared national champion – the post-season games hadn't yet counted in the final wire service polls – and was opposed by No. 2 Wisconsin. The rankings held up beautifully in one of the most exciting fourth quarter runs in Rose Bowl history as the Badgers, trailing 42-14, almost pulled off an upset by scoring the final 23 points.

This was McKay's first Rose Bowl game as head coach and he must have thought it was incredibly easy, as quarterback Pete Beathard threw four touchdown passes. Feeling the game was won, he shut down his passing offense, but Wisconsin quarterback Ron VanderKelen opened his up and

Southern Cal, which had maintained its national title in 1968 with a 14-3 victory over Indiana that was helped by O.J. Simpson's 128 yards and both touchdowns, lost a chance to wrestle one from Ohio State in 1969. USC was ranked second behind the Buckeyes, and though Simpson capped his Heisman Trophy year with 171 yards, including an 80-yard TD run that helped USC to a 10-0 lead, it wasn't enough. Helped by five USC turnovers and great running power, Ohio State prevailed 27-16.

There have been other trips to other bowls, but somehow it never has seemed anything but appropriate that the University of Southern California make that little trip to Pasadena – even if it does take three grueling months.

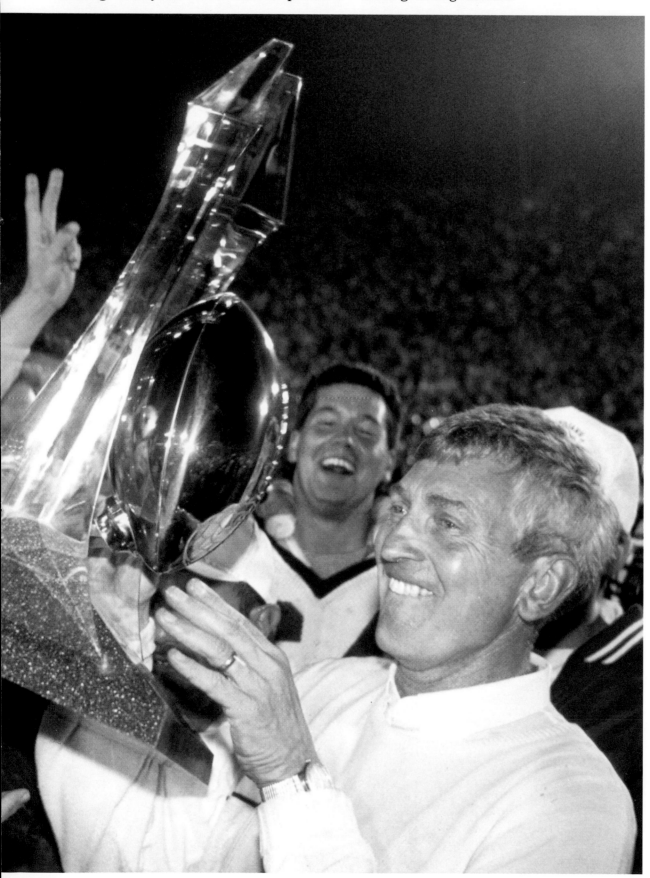

Left: *Coach Larry Smith holds up the 1990 Rose Bowl Trophy after USC beat Michigan 17-10.*

USC Trojans
Football Records

YEAR-BY-YEAR RESULTS

Year	Coach	W	L	T	Pts	Opp	Year	Coach	W	L	T	Pts	Opp
1888	A. Goddard,						1940	Howard Jones	3	4	2	88	98
	F. Suffell	2	0	0	20	0	1941	Sam Barry	2	6	1	64	134
1889	None	2	0	0	66	0	1942	Jeff Cravath	5	5	1	184	128
1890	No Team						1943	Jeff Cravath	8	2	0	155	58
1891	None	1	2	0	48	26	1944	Jeff Cravath	8	0	2	240	73
1892	No Team						1945	Jeff Cravath	7	4	0	205	150
1893	None	3	1	0	56	50	1946	Jeff Cravath	6	4	0	158	106
1894	None	1	0	0	12	0	1947	Jeff Cravath	7	2	1	193	114
1895	None	0	1	1	4	14	1948	Jeff Cravath	6	3	1	142	87
1896	None	0	3	0	0	44	1949	Jeff Cravath	5	3	1	214	170
1897	Harry Martin,						1950	Jeff Cravath	2	5	2	114	182
	Lew Freeman	5	1	0	100	18	1951	Jess Hill	7	3	0	224	168
1898	None	5	1	1	97	28	1952	Jess Hill	10	1	0	254	47
1899	None	2	3	1	11	33	1953	Jess Hill	6	3	1	199	161
1900	None	1	1	1	5	11	1954	Jess Hill	8	4	0	258	159
1901	Clair Tapaan	0	1	0	0	6	1955	Jess Hill	6	4	0	265	158
1902	None	2	3	0	29	44	1956	Jess Hill	8	2	0	218	126
1903	John Walker	4	2	0	58	27	1957	Don Clark	1	9	0	86	204
1904	Harvey Holmes	6	1	0	199	27	1958	Don Clark	4	5	1	151	120
1905	Harvey Holmes	6	3	1	211	45	1959	Don Clark	8	2	0	195	90
1906	Harvey Holmes	2	0	2	36	0	1960	John McKay	4	6	0	95	152
1907	Harvey Holmes	5	1	0	182	20	1961	John McKay	4	5	1	150	167
1908	Bill Traeger	3	1	1	63	18	1962	John McKay	11	0	0	261	92
1909	Dean Cromwell	3	1	2	133	13	1963	John McKay	7	3	0	207	114
1910	Dean Cromwell	7	0	1	189	24	1964	John McKay	7	3	0	207	130
1911-13	No Team						1965	John McKay	7	2	1	262	92
1914	Ralph Glaze	4	3	0	116	88	1966	John McKay	7	4	0	199	128
1915	Ralph Glaze	3	4	0	132	119	1967	John McKay	10	1	0	258	87
1916	Dean Cromwell	5	3	0	129	80	1968	John McKay	9	1	1	259	168
1917	Dean Cromwell	4	2	1	127	47	1969	John McKay	10	0	1	261	128
1918	Dean Cromwell	2	2	2	61	61	1970	John McKay	6	4	1	343	233
1919	Elmer Henderson	4	1	0	87	21	1971	John McKay	6	4	1	229	164
1920	Elmer Henderson	6	0	0	171	21	1972	John McKay	12	0	0	467	134
1921	Elmer Henderson	10	1	0	362	52	1973	John McKay	9	2	1	322	202
1922	Elmer Henderson	10	1	0	236	31	1974	John McKay	10	1	1	363	142
1923	Elmer Henderson	6	2	0	173	62	1975	John McKay	8	4	0	247	140
1924	Elmer Henderson	9	2	0	269	44	1976	John Robinson	11	1	0	386	139
1925	Howard Jones	11	2	0	456	55	1977	John Robinson	8	4	0	357	212
1926	Howard Jones	8	2	0	317	52	1978	John Robinson	12	1	0	318	153
1927	Howard Jones	8	1	1	287	64	1979	John Robinson	11	0	1	389	171
1928	Howard Jones	9	0	1	267	59	1980	John Robinson	8	2	1	265	134
1929	Howard Jones	10	2	0	492	69	1981	John Robinson	9	3	0	294	170
1930	Howard Jones	8	2	0	382	66	1982	John Robinson	8	3	0	302	143
1931	Howard Jones	10	1	0	363	52	1983	Ted Tollner	4	6	1	210	238
1932	Howard Jones	10	0	0	201	13	1984	Ted Tollner	9	3	0	220	173
1933	Howard Jones	10	1	1	257	30	1985	Ted Tollner	6	6	0	223	187
1934	Howard Jones	4	6	1	120	110	1986	Ted Tollner	7	5	0	264	239
1935	Howard Jones	5	7	0	155	124	1987	Larry Smith	8	4	0	321	229
1936	Howard Jones	4	2	3	129	65	1988	Larry Smith	10	2	0	370	184
1937	Howard Jones	4	4	2	136	98	1989	Larry Smith	9	2	1	336	132
1938	Howard Jones	9	2	0	172	65	1990	Larry Smith	8	4	1	348	274
1939	Howard Jones	8	0	2	181	33							

TOP CAREER RUSHERS

	Att	Yds	Avg
1. Charles White (1976-79)	1147	6245	5.44
2. Marcus Allen (1978-81)	932	4810	5.16
3. Anthony Davis (1972-74)	784	3724	4.75
4. Ricky Bell (1973-76)	710	3689	5.20
5. O. J. Simpson (1967-68)	674	3423	5.08

TOP CAREER RECEIVERS

	Rec	Yds	Avg	TD
1. John Jackson (1986-89)	163	2379	14.60	17
2. Eric Affholter (1985-88)	123	1737	14.12	13
3. Hank Norman (1982-85)	113	1731	15.32	6
4. Jeff Simmons (1980-82)	106	1826	17.22	11
5. Joe Cormier (1983-85)	105	1189	11.23	5

TOP CAREER PASSERS

	Att	Com	Yds	Td	Int
1. Rodney Peete (1985-88)	1081	630	8225	54	42
2. Todd Marinovich (1989-90)	674	415	5001	29	25
3. Sean Salisbury (1982-85)	602	346	4481	25	19
4. Paul McDonald (1977-79)	501	299	4138	37	13
5. Jim Jones (1969-71)	604	298	4092	30	25

CAREER TOTAL OFFENSE LEADERS

	Plays	Rush	Pass	Total
1. Rodney Peete (1985-88)	1371	415	8225	8640
2. Charles White (1976-79)	1149	6245	−5	6240
3. Marcus Allen (1978-81)	936	4810	57	4867
4. Jim Jones (1969-71)	842	409	4092	4501
5. Sean Salisbury (1982-85)	713	−354	4481	4127

BOWL RESULTS

The Aloha Bowl – Honolulu, Hawaii
Record: Won 0, Lost 1
1985 – Alabama 24, USC 3

The Astro-Bluebonnet Bowl – Houston, Texas
Record: Won 1, Lost 0
1977 – USC 47, Texas A&M 28

The Christmas Festival – Los Angeles, California
Record: Won 1, Lost 0
1924 – USC 20, Missouri 7

The Citrus Bowl – Orlando, Florida
Record: Won 0, Lost 1
1987 – Auburn 16, USC 7

The Fiesta Bowl – Tempe, Arizona
Record: Won 0, Lost 1
1982 – Penn State 26, USC 10

The John Hancock Bowl – El Paso, Texas
Record: Won 0, Lost 1
1990 – Michigan State 17, USC 16

The Liberty Bowl – Memphis, Tennessee
Record: Won 1, Lost 0
1975 – USC 20, Texas A&M 0

The Rose Bowl – Pasadena, California
Record: Won 19, Lost 8
1923 – USC 14, Penn State 3
1930 – USC 47, Pittsburgh 14
1932 – USC 21, Tulane 12
1933 – USC 35, Pittsburgh 0
1939 – USC 7, Duke 3
1940 – USC 14, Tennessee 0
1944 – USC 29, Washington 0
1945 – USC 25, Tennessee 0
1946 – Alabama 34, USC 14
1948 – Michigan 49, USC 0
1953 – USC 7, Wisconsin 0
1955 – Ohio State 20, USC 7
1963 – USC 42, Wisconsin 37
1967 – Purdue 14, USC 13
1968 – USC 14, Indiana 3
1969 – Ohio State 27, USC 16
1970 – USC 10, Michigan 3
1973 – USC 42, Ohio State 17
1974 – Ohio State 42, USC 21
1975 – USC 18, Ohio State 17
1977 – USC 14, Michigan 6
1979 – USC 17, Michigan 10
1980 – USC 17, Ohio State 16
1985 – USC 20, Ohio State 17
1988 – Michigan State 20, USC 17
1989 – Michigan 22, USC 14
1990 – USC 17, Michigan 10

Composite Bowl Record:
Won 22, Lost 12

Index

Page numbers in italics refer to illustrations